ne of your primary obligations on the earth plane is to take energy from the amazing sweeps of rarified spiritual power called the Vastness and bring it down into physical form, so It can have Its expression and Its understanding here. To remind you of this, I would like to speak about the last drama of the Christ. As one of the most compelling dramas of all time, you can place it in your awareness to help you journey Home. Let us remember what it was He did at the end of His life and why it serves today as a model for you.

There are very few human experiences as devastating or as painful as the one the Christos undertook at the crucifixion. In the midst of that event, with humiliation, ridicule, and disbelief added to intense physical pain, a cry went out. "Forgive them, they know not what they do." When he said this, do you think Jesus was talking to God? Could it be the Divine was not aware of the web of circumstances surrounding those last moments of His Beloved? Do you really feel that Jesus the man could have been aware of the need for forgiveness and the Divine was not?

If He was not speaking to God, let us ask to whom was He speaking? *The Christ was speaking to you and to everyone that has come to the earth plane after the moment of that plea*. Please dwell on this statement. It is the message of the cross. In your most extreme moments, your major obligation to yourself and to the wholeness of Life is to continue to manifest the love, beauty, power, and acceptance of your destiny as it is given to you. The Christ's was a victorious ending, achieved under the most dire of circumstances. If He can do it, I assure you He came to say, "So can you!"

Do not be separate from His teachings. When it enters your consciousness you can live from His point of power, it becomes the beginning of that reality. The path of the warrior is to know every event comes to remind you of why you are here: *To love to the best of your heart's ability, to be as accepting of all parts of your life as you possibly can, and to remember there is a Power that exists, without question, and It runs your life*. If you depend on It, as He did, you also will be carried Home. 🖋 *Bartholomew*

from the heart of a gentle brother

bartholomew

**HIGH MESA
PRESS
1987**

COVER AND DESIGN
Joy Franklin

EDITORS
Ashisha
Joy Franklin
Charles Josseph Rynear

Word Processing
Phyllis Johnson

Typesetting
WDType

Printed by
Braun Brumfield, Inc.

Informal tapes and transcripts of talks by
Bartholomew are available from
Dr. John Aiken
920 Annette St.
Socorro, NM 87801

Published by
High Mesa Press
P.O. Box 2267 Taos, NM 87571

To J., J., J., and L., for obvious reasons.
All Love, M.M.

nami (wave)

C O N T E N T S

O N E
PUBLIC SHARINGS

T W O
INDIVIDUAL AND GROUP EXERCISES

THREE
SYMBOLS, ALLIES AND MYTHS

> In order to activate a symbol so it can be use-
> ful, it is necessary to place that symbol outside
> of you so you can respond to it.

> All of the animal kingdoms have been doing
> an amazing job on behalf of the planet since
> its earliest days.

> There is written deeply within each of you, a
> wondrous myth that is your own.

FOUR
QUESTIONS AND ANSWERS

I · N · T · R · O · D

In the eight years that I have been doing this Bartholomew work, I have been asked a lot of questions. The ones most often asked are: "How could an educated and reasonably intelligent woman like you deal with being a psychic?" And "How did you come to know that you were really in touch with some awareness that was different from your own?" And lastly, "How have you dealt with the huge changes that this lifestyle has brought?" The answers are so different than what they were eight years ago, the only way to be clear is to begin at the beginning and try to show their unfoldment.

So, what of that first year, the months following the day that, under medical hypnosis, I ran into the energy vortex we have come to call Bartholomew?

Physical difficulties carried Mary-Margaret to Socorro, New Mexico, to visit old friends Doctors John and Louisa Aiken. They believed in relaxation through hypnosis, so Dr. John Aiken recommended it as a technique to relieve the pain of her back problems. He started with a mental suggestion. "Go down a hallway and open the door." She did. The door opened into a past life and Mary-Margaret was overcome by a totally new feeling. The energy we call Bartholomew started talking to Dr. Aiken.

I would describe that year as one of interest and excitement combined with equal portions of panic. My background had been strongly Zen, which emphasizes the impermanence of all things, and certainly does not recommend letting such a thing as this Bartholomew experiment become too important. The Zen masters all admit that such things are possible, but they strongly suggest you view them simply as passing clouds of not much importance. The goal of Zen is the awareness of that which is beyond all name and form. So, my first reaction to having Bartholomew arrive on

U · C · T · I · O · N

the scene was, "Let's get all of the information we can from this energy in as short a period of time as possible and then drop it, and back to za-zen." Well obviously, that did not happen and it is because I began to experience the *usefulness* of this energy, both for me and for others. I saw, time after time, that this energy did have a vaster point of view, that it could "see things we could or would not see," and sharing that made a difference in terms of helping us change our limited points of view. It did seem to be what it claimed, an elder brother who just wanted to help out.

In that first year, fear was often present. I was afraid I was operating under some grand ego illusion that would end up plunging me into a karmic mess that would take lifetimes to pull out of. So, in working with this fear, I decided to deal with it in various ways, and with as much *consciousness* as possible.

First and foremost, I decided to stand responsible for the validity of all of the information that was being given, to whatever extent that I could. If, for example, Bartholomew said an event would take place, then it was my intention and responsibility to follow up and verify if it indeed did happen. If suggestions were made that were to help one's spiritual unfoldment as a seeker, *did they work* as stated? Was there a change? It was very clear to me, and still is, that we have no reason to believe any psychic, myself included, unless the material available for checking on the 'earth plane' can be validated.

Mary-Margaret Moore

ii

If we can see the information proves truthful, clear, and helpful, then it seems to me that we have some basis for believing all of the material they give us about the 'unseen worlds,' about the journey Home, about our past lives, all of that. So this became my primary aim. I carefully watched the workings of this process and, as the years went by and the energy chalked up what I would call clarity after clarity, I began to relax and to allow myself to acknowledge that the information, the world view, indeed the cosmic view being presented, might be valid.

The second way of overcoming the fear was the use of the *I Ching*[1], that ancient Chinese book of changes. It became my cross-check for all of this process. Now, please realize I had worked for years with this amazingly difficult yet awesome text and had found it to be, if properly and patiently used, one of the clearest voices of truth that I had at hand. So time and time again, I turned to the *I Ching* for guidance. Question: How should I view the phenomenon called Bartholomew and our workings together? Answer: First hexagram, The Creative: "In relation to the universe, this hexagram expresses the strong creative action of the Deity. In relation to the human world, it denotes the creative action of the holy man or sage, of the ruler or leader of men, who through his power awakens and develops their higher nature." Again, another throw. Hexagram #14, Possession in Great Measure, nine at the top: "In the fullness of possession and at the height of power, one remains modest and gives honor to the sage who stands outside the affairs of the world." And finally, the one that most filled me with peace, hexagram #50, The Caldron. Supreme good fortune, six in the fifth place: "The ting has yellow handles. In the language of symbols this means a great deal. The line is the ruler of the hexagram and has over it a sage with whom it is connected by position and complementary relationship. The ruler is 'hollow' (receptive), hence capable of receiving the power, that is, the teachings of this sage. Thereby he makes progress."

The third way of overcoming the fear was really very practical. I paid attention to how I, and others who were listening, were feeling in their lives and what I saw was peace-producing. We were becoming stronger, fuller, more alive, and most of all, less fearful.

"By their fruits ye shall know them." And the fruits of decreasing fear and a stronger sense of hope and peace seemed, even to my doubting mind, to have validity.

But how does a graduate of a Stanford University Graduate School bridge the gap between "rational mind" and "Big Mind?" Well, it was the same process as above. In time, *doing* what was suggested, *listening* with inner awareness, and then *watching* how that inner awareness worked in the world became my criteria. Was my rational mind any better at helping me out? No. Did there have to be a choice between both parts of me? No. I found I could use both tools, the "rational mind" for rational things, and "Big Mind" for big things. And what are these big things? Things like letting go of fear, understanding the nature of pain and how to deal with it, finding separation dropping from my awareness and a kind of wholeness coming in its place, and perhaps most magical of all, feeling the beginnings of that sought after wonder, love. Not just for those that are my beloveds, but Love—unspecified, without object. And a few times, by the grace of the Unknown, without subject. I delight in having had a good strong academic education, for it has brought me tremendous joy. But I am also incredibly grateful "rational mind" is not the only mind alive and well in our universe.

So, for the final question, how do I deal with my lifestyle, a lifestyle that was certainly not a conscious choice of mine, and a lifestyle that quite often pulls me out of the mainstream of the world and puts me in some other kind of flow? The answer, honestly given, is that being out of the mainstream doesn't seem to matter. Yes, I am seen by some as a freak, a fraud, a nut, or at worst, a devil. But those are other people's words, and they do not feel real to me when I contemplate them within myself. And I do contemplate them within myself, for I feel it is also part of my responsibility to listen to what is given, to internalize it as a working power and to decide whether it rings true for me or whether it does not. What *are* real are the feelings of love, peace, and gratitude that are building in me year after year as I attempt to carry out my part of this experiment. And I am delighted to remember it *is* an experiment, a wonderful, organic process of unfoldment,

iv

extension and creation. It isn't something static I have to fill the form of but rather a process that I am a part of. In the end, you know, I am the laboratory of this experiment, so I have to look to the laboratory for proof of the worthwhileness of the whole attempt.

I find I am not the same person I was before this began. I am no longer afraid of what the future might hold, not only for me but for the world and all of us in it, because I now feel one overriding thing to be true. We are part of a protective power of a Reality that Cares, that intimately, intensely, and continuously Cares. We have, each of us, an inner 'something' which guides us every moment we choose to turn our awareness to it and listen. We are, all of us, participating in a glorious expansion of awareness both mysterious and awesome. We are not what we think ourselves to be. We are so much, much more and so much, much greater than our limited minds would have us believe. We are a part of the Vastness in some wondrous way and it is our Life's delight to find out this is so. I cannot thank Life enough for the opportunity to awaken, to awaken to the fullness of Who We Are, and for the incredible joy that awakening brings.

Mary-Margaret Moore

[1]*Richard Wilhelm*, The I Ching, *Princeton University Press, Princeton, New Jersey, 1977.*

Part One
PUBLIC SHARINGS

One of the truths Bartholomew occasionally reminds us of
goes like this: "When two or more are gathered...," and
sometimes ends by saying "magic happens." And
'magic' in its highest form is truly what happens
when Bartholomew shares with groups of
people. Everyone partakes of the combined
energies present and all leave expanded
to some extent. The following material
has been selected from the public
sharings held over the past few
years. We invite you now to
participate in the Wisdom
and Love of our brother,
Bartholomew.

equality; peace

First Sharing
February 24, 1985
Albuquerque, New Mexico

A FOOT
IN BOTH WORLDS

*For the past several months,
we have shared from a level
of understanding based on
the receptivity of the human
body. And I have asked that
you remember that the body
itself is in the process of
building new systems to
receive new energies. This
morning we will talk
about those systems.*

he New Age is a very blasé subject now, but if you will contemplate deeply what new means, you will realize we are talking about changing the old to receive the new. The difficulty with the reception of the new lies within the physical body itself. New inroads need to be *consciously* created. You cannot remain unconscious about the process and have this new, wondrous energy come pouring through your physical being as fast as you would wish it to. Many of the difficulties you are experiencing in the physical, emotional, and even the mental sense, come from the inability of the body to truly receive and move with what is now happening in your life. And when the movement through the physical is difficult, it can be jarring. Relationships that were pleasing no longer fill you, jobs that were satisfying are harder to move through, and inner clarity still eludes you. Things like these are simply signals to tell you that *now* is the time to consider how to make these inroads so that all the clarity, wisdom, and health you seek will be yours.

If you wish to be a receiver and holder of this energy, please understand your end of the commitment. It is simply this: to watch yourself constantly, with detached observation—to see what illumines and ignites you, and to see what deadens you. You have been running on past information for many years. You can no longer do things by rote. To say that you've always done things a certain way and so proceed with your life is no longer applicable. What is called for now is a *total action*. You can enlighten yourself with the awareness that the new is ever present by keeping watch in your own physical, mental, emotional, and spiritual laboratory.

For example, if you find yourself going daily to a job that deadens you, you might consider changing it. If you find yourself with people that you resist being with, instead of continually adjusting those relationships, you might consider it time to weed them out of your life. And when you do, my friends, please *do not fill those places until you know you are filling them with the power of the new* instead of the repetition of the old. The human psyche is afraid of emptiness. You are *afraid* of the vast wonder that opens you to your Being, so you fill your days and nights with outside events. And because of this, when the new energy caresses you,

1

there is no room for it. You are filled with thoughts and actions that no longer bring power to your life. So when we talk about the new, you must understand to create the new, you let go of the old.

This new energy is pouring into the earth and far past it. It is not just this little planet that is going to be engulfed with wonder. There is a vast area in this part of the universe that is going to be lifted and *is* being lifted into another state of understanding. Change is upon the face of this earth, and the outward manifestations of physical change mirror the inner changes that are occurring and will occur in the psyche and the physical body. With them, you are presented with a very basic, helpful tool that can change your life. You have the opportunity of using yourself as an ongoing, *conscious* receptor of this power. You can be the receptor by sending out the call constantly: "Fill me, make me whole. Do whatever transmutation this body needs to have done to make me alive and aware. Help me." Or you can keep on stumbling through your life, trying to fix those areas that are constantly falling apart.

Each one of you has deeply recorded in your psyche an incredibly empowered statement of desire. "*I want to be*! I want to be free. I want to be one with God. I want to feel total compassion. I want to be loving." *You* know what to ask for. And if you can clarify what you really want for yourself once and for all, and keep that desire as a constant focus, *you will receive what you seek.* You cannot submerge yourself in the mundane world, becoming transfixed by the manipulations of the earth plane, and at the same time be receptive to this power. *Now is the time of choice* and the choices you make are important. By the power of your psyche's deepest desire, you will be changed. That has always been the promise. Seek ye first the kingdom, and the rest will come. Please understand my desperation, because those of you who are caught, who are not willing to take your attention off the mundane life, are going to find yourselves in difficulty. Your bodies will be in trauma and your minds in confusion.

Many of you are tired of changing the surface of your life and want changes to come from the depths of your being. You have tried all the worldly ways, have you not? You have meditated in a hundred positions, gone to a hundred therapists, and although some changes have taken place, inside yourself you feel incomplete. Your life has still not been ignited. What, then, to do?

If you are ready and committed to giving the attention and awareness necessary, you can begin to change to your psyche's deepest desire. You can be open and alive to it or become closed and fight it. The power is coming and the leading edge is here! You cannot put rules on energy. Each of you has the ability to empower the psychic field around you by putting out the call that will draw the energy to you. You have asked for change, so do not try to negotiate your way through it. As the energy enters, outer forms will begin to fall away. Things that seemed very permanent will be eased from your life, and out of fear you may try to resist them, replace them, or substitute other things for them.

Instead of succumbing to fear, may I suggest an alternative, a shift in awareness? There is a part in all of you that few of you have taken the time to develop because it is not lucrative to do so. But in the last rounds of the incarnative cycle, the main commitment is not in working the material plane. The commitment is to yourself, to be aware and alive to yourself every day, and to bring into form, *your inner truth*. YOUR inner truth. You have been a nation, indeed a planet, that spends a lot of time listening to others' opinions. And what is necessary is to spend time listening to yourself. *You* know what makes you sing, what makes you dance and laugh and love. But if you do not ask yourself what it is that you know, you will go on listening to others, and change will not come because you will not hear your own truth. Every day you spend time taking care of other people, and who is the one that is ignored? Your Self! Sit down and ask yourself what would delight *you*. These next several years are going to be wonderful for those of you who want the movement that changes bring. It is the creative side of you that makes your life worth living! That outreaching, creative side is the part that inspires you, that explodes you into your own truth day by day. So spend time every day listening to what your muse is trying to tell you. There are artists of one kind or another inside *all* of you, but because you have had to focus on making the world sensible, practical and usable, those abilities are

3

just orphans sitting in the back of your life. Understand that you are wondrously complex beings. And when you live on the earth plane, you have to focus to get things done. Please consider widening the focus. Listen with your Being, and the more you listen, the more you will trust. The more you trust, the more you will expand. And the more you expand, the happier you will be and around it will go.

Over two thousand years ago the world was in a position similar to the one it is in today. The polarities were there, the differences were there, the belief structures were firmly in place, and everyone knew just what to do in order to be 'right.' If you believed in yourself enough to listen to yourself, you would realize that now is the time to become your own oracle. Ask yourself what you want, what you need, and then move into it and try it. It's a time of trial. You're going to fall on your face now and then, so pick yourself up and try something else. To tune into this energy, you are going to have to develop a new set of ears. You are used to listening to the buzz of the world, but now is the time to develop the inner ear that listens to the inner world. It is time to have a foot in each world, and it can be done!

Living the Life Divine is learning to live with the awareness of your inner power and to translate it through the physical body and out into the earth plane. So set your goal to *listen*. To listen with more and more of your being so that you can sit in the most abysmal circumstances and feel alive and safe and well. That feeling of safety does not come from paying attention to the world. It comes from learning how to be the arbiter between the Vastness and the mundane. It's an amazingly beautiful job, to bring the Divine down to this planet and anchor it in everything you do and say and look upon. You consciously allow yourself to feel the Divine and in doing so silently remind others you and they are It!

A long, long time ago, you left the space of Unity and moved into the plane of duality. That was not a voyage that you had a choice about. You did it because you needed to. The yearning inside your being for something vaster is the call from the deepest part of your soul that now wants to end this experiment in duality and move into union. But, my friends, making this a planet

4

of unity is difficult—that is not why it was created. You are trying to do something to this wonderful planet that it doesn't need to have done. There are billions upon billions of people who are learning maximum lessons through how they function here. Many of you have learned that you no longer feel alive by killing, that joy comes from sharing not from owning, that peace is found within and is not dependent on others. Do not condemn the planet for being what it is. It is a wondrous teacher. *Your* responsibility is to end the duality *in yourself.* And that end will come from the integration of all the parts of you.

All around you people are yearning for change. That is the outward sign of a coming spiritual grace. Understand that you can go anywhere you want and the energy will find you. Please consider the wonder of this opportunity. You cannot miss. You were not wrong to pick this time. But *now is the time!* The longer you continue to stay focused on the world, forcing it to feed you the happiness that you are seeking, the longer you will be frustrated. The part of your soul that wants to be filled with something else is not going to be satisfied if your awareness is focused primarily 'out there.' You must learn to be the interface between the worlds and have those worlds connect in your life in the most wondrous ways that you can. Ask to be filled with those things the Soul longs for. Keep on asking for love, compassion, peace, and joy. *Then put your awareness in your heart center, and feel them.*

Every time you do feel a shift in the energy within your physical body, acknowledge it. Please acknowledge that something has happened. This is the time to empower your Being, and the more of you that do, the greater the service you render to each other. Please think about it. You have asked to be sent an energy that will once and for all change and transmute your cloudy projections and illusions to true perception and clarity. You have asked to be in the world and carry out your duties, and at the same time to also be alive and ignited with the knowledge of your true Being. The difference between twenty years ago and now is that the energy is here. And it's going to get stronger. So allow things to fall away and change before your eyes. Just keep moving. Know that whatever leaves, no matter how deeply you cared about it,

5

how attached you were, or how meaningful it was, is appropriate. The next movement will always appear.

In times past, it was possible to listen to the organizations of the world and to feel strong, but the organizations are now failing. Governments are being seen as less than perfect. Religions are unable to fill you with the power of the Divine. And that is all absolutely as it should be. If life becomes chaotic, do not despair, but remember that *your life is your responsibility*. And also please remember you began this journey with the knowledge that, if you could open to your Vaster Self, you would have available at every moment the information necessary to empower your inner and outer life. The 'other' world is totally porous, and it moves through everything. Its wisdom is ever present and ever available.

When you listen to yourself and your truths begin to unfold, do not immediately present them to the world because discouragement committees will form to dissuade you. That change is exciting, uplifting and delightful is not something the world is ready to hear. So be very gentle with those around you. Hold them in deep consideration and understanding. And if, by the power of your love through your changes, you can move those wonderful feelings out into the world, those around you will know that there is no harm in them. Change accomplished through the power of your inner Being is absolutely peace-filled. It is so because it moves out of a place of knowing, not out of a place of fear. The wonderful excitement of listening to yourself is that you know what is right when you hear it, and when your movement comes out of an inner knowing, it rings with truth, and that certainty brings peace to you, and those around you.

Q: How, in the process of trying to listen to something vaster, do you deal with the negative patternings that come up?

My friend, I think you will find that your mind can only concentrate on one thing at a time. So when negative patterns arise, you will see that *there is a moment of choice*. You can, by your own sweet will, choose to ask for something besides your old patterns. You can allow the new to enter if you do not continually try to dissect, re-evaluate and analyze the darkness of the past. Once you have really decided that the negative pattern is not

6

getting you what you want, you will choose to change it. When you shift your focus, your mind will begin to create new patterns. You stay with negative thoughts because you think that if you paw through the garbage can long enough you are going to find a pearl. When you finally decide it is much more likely you will find a pearl in the ocean, you will cease looking in the garbage can. Just keep asking or praying for the awareness, the shift into light and expansion. Be in control of your consciousness, for when you are, negativity has to leave. Negativity is an energy vortex which you keep recreating. You cannot transform that kind of energy and you don't need to. Leave it alone. Just acknowledge the feelings and drop them. Leave the garbage can. Decide to go for a swim.

Do something different. *Ask to expand.* You will begin to pull a different energy vortex into your physical body. We are talking about a cellular, physical energy change. The experience will be wonderful. You will feel lightness and be joy-filled. When you speak to others, you will not be in a state of tension and defense, but will speak with openness and wonder. Now is the time. A change, to be truly a change, has to shift your entire psyche. It has to change the totality of your Being. Before you entered this earth plane, you made a contract that, when you called for it, the power to make those changes would arrive. When you were ready to leave, the 'ship' would be there. My friends, many of you are ready for a new experience. So please choose and then test what you have heard. Do not dwell on what negative things might happen, just keep doing the only job that you have, which is to ground the Light on this planet by making it alive *in you.*

You are not alone. Everyone that has ever walked this blessed planet knows the difficulties that the physical, splintered psyche produces. Their power, their awareness, and their compassion are still available to you. Of the millions who have released themselves from this limited state of awareness, many have chosen to assist. When you call, you will be answered. When you ask to be filled with a consciousness that will allow you to love everything you see and every thought you think, it will begin to happen. You have never been alone, but the present wonder is that we are now closer to you. And we are very grateful this is so.

Second Sharing
December 16, 1985
Albuquerque, New Mexico

HARMLESSNESS

This is the time that you have come to call the Christmas season, and I would like to participate with you in a little different way than usual.

I have been asked a compelling question by many people. If it is true this is a planet of polarity, and if it is true there are other states of consciousness that allow for a greater understanding of Being, what then is required to move into that new consciousness?

I would like to bring forth a possibility. Please stop now and close your eyes. Put aside all of your preconceived ideas for awhile and put yourself into an energy field with as few impressions in it as possible. Just take a moment to imagine a softly moving energy field that allows itself to be permeated by new concepts.

The reason you are not instantly enlightened by concepts is because your vibrational frequency contains energy fields which are incompatible with each other. Simply stated, you want the new, but you don't want to let go of the old, so you have to hear the new concept again and again before you allow it to permeate your auric field. You are permeable beings and you can become more permeable at any moment, because it is a matter of choice. So, if you would like to receive a gift from yourself, choose to become permeable now.

As high a truth as I can bring to you this day is the understanding that, in order to move to another level of awareness, another expression of Being, *you do not have to be in a state of total enlightenment.* You do not have to be an Avatar or think only loving, uplifting, wondrous thoughts, or perform the actions of saints. But there is one thing that you absolutely must contain, which is a state of *51% harmlessness.*

Why harmlessness, why not love? My friends, with all due respect for your capacities to love, you've got a lot to learn. You are on your way to uncovering all the parts of your Being, so please realize the pale replica you call love on this earth plane has, as its reality, incredible extensions of wonder and power, far past your own present ideas. Be grateful you are on your way. If you like what you are experiencing now, think what you will be experiencing when you truly are in the state of Love?

To understand harmlessness, let us use some symbology. You have in your minds the awareness of a point of what you call critical mass. That is, you have two potentially unstable elements. You add one small component that is insignificant in itself and the entire thing moves into tremendous exploding power. The earth plane is symbolic in this way. You have been asking for a maximum explosion in your consciousness, and you have every right to believe it can happen when you look at the world as symbolic. The example is there. Nuclear explosions have something to say that can be positive in a very personal way. Be aware that you do not create such events only for your negative understanding. You also create them for your positive absorption of truth. The explosion of consciousness you are looking for comes when that one additional something is added to create critical mass. *Harmlessness* is that one additional something.

So why 51%? The extra 1% is what boosts you into true harmlessness. On other planes of consciousness, when your mind creates an event, it manifests instantly, and therefore you stand immediately responsible for what you have created. Because you would be able, *at a thought*, to destroy others and then have to come back and somehow 'pay' for that experience, some rules have been set and you have agreed to them. You have agreed not to be let into these instantly creative areas until you have learned not to hurt yourselves or others. It is of no help to play in those realms of consciousness where you would accumulate difficult 'karma' for yourselves. What is helpful is to state the entrance requirements and remind you that you are absolutely capable of meeting them because you have helped to create them.

How then do you become harmless? You begin by becoming harmless to yourself. Many of you have been trained to figure out what others want and then to satisfy their needs. But the day will come when you awaken and realize that, because of the trade-offs, you don't know what *you* want or who *you* are. And some of the responses that come with that realization are harmful to yourself and others. You cannot give harmless recognition to anyone else until you recognize the harmlessness of your own Self, and you go about it by deeply realizing that *you truly have nothing to fear.* When you have nothing to fear, you do not have to defend and you do not have to attack. You will not need other people to see you as perfect, and you will allow yourself to say your own truth, be your own truth, and live your own truth. You cannot feel secure in yourself until you know that you are not threatened by the choices of others.

So the dilemma is to move in the world in a way that will not bring harm. And since the solution lies within you, to discover

10

it, sit quietly with yourself and feel the energies in and about you, without any kind of judgment. When you do this on a daily basis, you will begin to feel *the dependability and power of your own energy.* You are powerful beings and have the ability to experience the reality of the 'foreground' and 'background' of who you are. The foreground, or front of your body, is very active, while the back of it is receptive to the Source. As you sit and experience this, you begin to see you can activate both of them simultaneously, you do not have to jump from one to the other, and you can blend them moment by moment.

Every moment you walk around in a body you have access to the background, to the Source, because it is a part of you. Harmlessness comes through the experience of *knowing* that whatever you are doing, you are *simultaneously* touching upon the Power that knows what right action is and will, if you allow it, perform through you. You have the idea that you live only out of the front part of your being. That is a lie. You are constantly being pushed from behind. Some of you have lived through tremendous difficulties and, looking back, wonder how you overcame them. All of the time the unseen has been moving, pushing, and showing you other choices. You are not aware of the constant promptings of the Source, so you are not alive to them.

How do you become alive to these promptings? How do you become alive to anything? The only way is to address them, to turn your awareness to them, to begin to communicate with them on an active basis. This means that you are not involved only in the external frontal movement, but are aware of the internal back. You cannot have a friend in alliance with you, helping you, unless you *turn to them* and ask. Many of you are waiting for something that very few of you are going to get. You are waiting to be absorbed by some wonderful cosmic 'Being' of whatever shape your mind has decided will appear. But the gods will not dance in your living room, showing you their beauty, and then tell you to go back to the garbage heap. Some of the God-like openings that you get are assurances of the existence of a greater reality, but the job of finishing up whatever it is you have come to do remains. The aim is *not* to have the gods dance in your living room, my friends. The

11

aim is to have *harmlessness* dancing in your being, deeply and clearly! This is very possible. Fifty-one percent for many of you is not far away. But 50% is not 51%. And being almost there isn't good enough.

You know in your being whether each action you perform is harmless or if it is not. And if it is harmful, the point is to understand why you *want* to be harmful, not to judge against your harmfulness. How can you be harmless when inside of your being there is unfinished material that you have yet to work with? If you feel yourself rising up in harmfulness against someone, ask yourself *why*. If your goal is to be harmless, then what is this action saying to you? What can you do to understand it *now*? Do not leap over it. You will defeat yourself. You have to get down to the level that acknowledges you are acting in a harmful way and find out why you are afraid. You do not act harmfully unless you are afraid. Harmlessness comes from *not* being afraid of whatever is happening in the moment.

When you become responsible for your actions often enough and see through the projection of your fears clearly enough, you will become harmless. If enough of you become 51% harmless, you will also be able to achieve that critical mass for your planet. If you cannot, it is because the majority does not wish it and the planet will do what the majority wants. The future of the earth cannot be foretold because at any time 51% can be reached and it will change with the consciousness of those on this planet. Critical mass happens in an instant. Your job is to make very sure what side you are on.

Who is to say, for example, whether all of the terrible starvation going on in parts of this and other countries is not doing something to help move you toward critical mass? You do not yet see or act out of acceptance of a larger plan for this world. So your job, every time you find yourself engaged in action, speech, or thought with another, is to find out if you are being harmless. If you are not, do not say it is their problem. Find out what is wrong in you and don't worry about what is out there! One of the reasons you are delaying reaching your own critical mass is that you keep trying to solve other people's dilemmas. That does not

12

help you or them. Judgment from a superior place creates in the other a feeling of tremendous defeat. *Superiority is a very bad exchange for God-realization.* The issue is simple. "Do unto others as you would have them do unto you." If you would not want to be treated thusly, then do not treat others that way. You know when you open your mouth whether you are speaking for yourself in the limited sense or for your Self in the vaster sense. You will eventually choose the Vastness, not because you are told to, but because you will recognize it as best for *your* well-being. Harmlessness is absolutely necessary for traversing from your current state of awareness to a vaster one.

If you want to get yourself to a state of Freedom as quickly as possible, I suggest that you be very serious about what we have shared. Find out those things you know you have been doing in your thoughts, words, and deeds that are harmful to others. Then, without judgment, be responsible for the choices you make. Harmlessness is felt when safety is present and safety feels present when you know you are not going to be attacked.

Many of you experience this feeling of safety with a few people, but do not feel safe with the rest of the world. If you are in a state of harmlessness, then in almost every instance you will attract to you the same quality. This is a universe of equals, and wherever you are on this reverberating scale of vibration, so you find those that play at much the same level. Yes, there are times when, by choice, you will move to other vibrational frequencies to allow things to happen because of your need to understand some part of yourself. And this usually means moving to a lower frequency range. You do not draw to you things that you do not need. To go around hiding yourself from the world because you are afraid of being hurt is one of the best ways to be hurt. Harmlessness comes from trusting yourself, from acknowledging your own trustworthiness, and therefore pulling into your life matching energies of trustworthiness. Together, you create a greater area of trust which in turn pulls more to it in ever increasing circles. *Critical mass for yourself comes from watching, acknowledging, and releasing anything that you see to be harmful.* Harmlessness on a worldly scale comes from the increased power generated as more harmless areas come together, until at some moment its critical mass occurs.

My friends, I cannot give you the gift of saying this planet will create such a critical mass. But I can tell you that if it doesn't, it will be because at least 51% didn't want it to. For those of you that do, you have my word that your state of awareness will be held intact, and you will find a way to leave the planet. But the gift we all can share is the knowledge that *your critical mass is in your hands.* Freedom lies in every moment, because you have freedom of choice. Alive mastery comes from being alive every moment to what you are doing, thinking or feeling. It is in your hands. You will never know when that moment of 51% will happen until you are there. All you can do is keep that desire as a clear and constant beacon in your consciousness. And the explosion will come! *You* are in control of your critical mass and every moment counts.

It is early February 1986. A group of twenty-eight seekers/finders are seated on the deck of a small boat adrift on the Sea of Galilee.[1] *They have spent many days together, differing in many ways, but united in one—the desire to answer the question: How can I, in the midst of seeming separation which brings pain, come to the place where I see only One— One world, One life, One Being, One God?*

The answer is to begin, this moment, *to live inside your Beingness.* As you move through the world, constantly go inward to check out your awareness. Take the power you have placed outside yourself and place it within. When you no longer follow the rules out there, the rules of your ego, or the rules of your desires, the peace that you have been looking for will become a reality. It is a courageous way to live because it means that you are willing to stand totally responsible for everything you choose.

You have a place of knowingness inside of you. You pretend you do not because your ego wants what it wants. But, in the end, what you really desire is to increase the love in your heart and the beautiful peace-filled feeling of right action in your life. This is what will make you happiest. Your ego is a temporary misconception, and, if you are watching your life carefully, you will realize that all of those things you so yearned for, and went ahead and manifested, did not provide you with any deep, lasting satisfaction. The process around ego desire goes on endlessly. If your single-pointed desire is to live inside yourself and know clearly what actions are selfless, harmless, and loving, then, *without any other goal*, you will achieve what you call enlightenment. But if you think you have other goals just as important, then you will have to follow the turn of what you call the karmic wheel. If the eye be single, then your Being is whole. When your single goal is peace through everything you do, you will achieve it.

Being the warrior means taking the risk of leaving the rules behind and deciding once and for all that the only criteria for living is the one that comes from your inner teacher. *No one can answer for you.* No one! You must answer for yourself and in the next moment be totally responsible for your choices. If you make an adjustment, and if it seems that it has been a selfish one, stand ready to learn, ask yourself to let go of it completely, and realize that it is part of the process of becoming whole. No guilt. No blame. No manipulation. Just letting go, acknowledging the lesson presented and moving on.

I am calling you to a very high task, because it takes constant awareness to live this way. It takes constant remembrance that the teacher is within, so you have to learn to *be still and know* that the teacher is present. You have to learn to live your life so that you are listening within, no matter what you are doing. That is the highest calling that you can answer to. In the end, it is the only thing that brings abiding peace, continuous love, and the wonder of knowing the light is you. That light shines out and flows where it needs to, so judge it not. *You are all in a state of becoming and at the same time you are all already totally filled with Being.*

Done with awareness, life is letting go of fears, letting go of guilt, letting go of limitations, letting go of ideas that trap you in the patterns of habit and do not leave you free to be spontaneous in the moment. I have begged you to think about spontaneity, how to live life with spontaneous wonder in a way that is harmless and whole at the same time. That, to me, is living the Life Divine. You cannot know what the Divine wants of you until the moment the choice is offered. Until that time, it is mentalization, the past, other people, remembrances, limitations. So the only place to live is in the spontaneous now. That is the only place that you can find right action, right speech, right love.

Remember—you came to bring, into the physical body of this wonderful createdness, a power that would allow you to live life more boldly, with greater awareness, and with a deep knowing that every step takes you Home. When all the rest has faded, remember the power within you. Instead of going to the mind, which gives you repetitive patterns of behavior, go inside to the energy within. Do not dissipate that energy in the same patterns you have lived before. When you believe the teacher is within and can speak to you in words you can understand, enlightenment is a short step away.

I am grateful to all of you. I am grateful for your hardships. I am grateful for your joys and for your sorrows. I am mostly grateful because, in your willingness to be warriors, you have created extra energy that I can take to wherever it is needed. And please don't ever forget how very loved you are, how totally and completely loved you all are. It has been my great delight to be with you, so please, since you wish to delight me also, take me with you. Keep me close so that I may have the joy of being with you, and hopefully you will have the equal joy of being with me.

---

[1]*Inward Bound Tours are composed of groups of people seeking their spiritual awakening, who spend two or three weeks touring parts of the globe that Bartholomew feels have transformative power. Bartholomew is available for one hour each day to maximize these opportunities. The tours are arranged by Friends of Vista Grande, P.O. Box 1656, Taos, New Mexico 87571.*

Third Sharing
February 23, 1986
Albuquerque, New Mexico

THE CHALLENGER AND THE CHALLENGE

On January 28, 1986, the United States launched its most ambitious space probe. Five men and two women made up the crew of the spacecraft Challenger. At 11:39 a.m. Eastern Standard Time, the Challenger roared into the skies above Cape Kennedy and moments later exploded before the horrified view of millions who witnessed the event on world-wide television. The shock of that disaster was felt for months as a grief-stricken nation asked "why?"

n the last few weeks, I have received many requests for clarification of the events surrounding the Challenger and what they must mean for your nation, and even past that, for the world itself.

Please understand before we begin that your present viewpoint is limited by your physical and mental bodies. You limit your viewpoints on purpose because part of your job is to take the very highest God-like power and manifest it in the world through the 'equipment' in your bodies. This is not a mistake, and I salute you for your courage. Nevertheless, when events such as the Challenger happen, and you only have your physical body and mental ideas to work with, you tend to view them in a linear way. Cause and effect move in a linear direction. But Creation is not linear, it is explosive. Events open up and fit together in a much broader pattern than most people are aware of at this time. So when you take an event such as Challenger and ask what it means, you also ask for an understanding of the total explosion of Creation and how wondrously more important and vast every event is.

When you use only your mind for understanding, you end up with limitation. Happenings such as the destruction of Challenger are too large in scope to fit in the confines of the mind. You have areas of awareness all around and through you which are constantly giving you ideas and promptings that come from the other parts of the psyche. These areas are not available to you on a physical, conscious level. So, as we talk, please try to rest in those parts of your Being that are vaster so that you can see what we present to you today is just *one* idea. There are many, many reasons for all of the events that happen in your life. If you say the earth plane only follows a line of karmic reality, you are looking at a very low model of Creation. Karmic reality is true in a limited way, but it is not the only truth and it is not the total truth.

So, let us expand our view around the Challenger by asking about the *motive* behind the action. When the motive is clear and true, you can rest assured that the results will not be harmful. So before we can go any further, we have to ask what the motive of the United States was in going out into space. Did it feel it was an important and necessary action, and did it also go because it

19

wanted to capture the attention of the world, perhaps to appear more powerful than another nation, the Soviet Union? So which motive was the greater?

One wonderful thing about the entire space program is the symbolic statement it makes about what mankind wants to do. Mankind desires to reach those deep parts of itself and wants to move out and become vaster. What is also necessary is to realize that the *outward* journey towards Vastness needs to be balanced by the *inward* journey towards Vastness. Space is an outward and visible hope of what you are looking for. But in the end, that which is within you has to be looked at.

The world, as it is presented to you today, is filled with needs, with longings, with desperate calls for help. In response to any of these could have come the help of an incredibly powerful nation which said, "We will do whatever we can here first, and when our home is in perfect harmony, beauty and wonder, then we will go out into the rest of the world and past the world to see what we can learn from there." You all know that there were many warning signals sent about the January launch. The intuition of the people in charge said that it should not go and they knew it. The signs were there clearly and powerfully. But because of pressures, the scope of which are hard to understand, they overrode their intuitive responses and let the Challenger go.

The lesson on the earth plane is very simple. If you do not listen to your own intuitive promptings, you, too, will launch things that will work against you. Your intuition leads you truly, but what happens is that you override it. You override it when you want to please other people, and when you keep your objectives linear. You stop listening to the intuitive and end up doing those things others say you *should* do. The Challenger is symbolic in this way. The intuition of many people said, "No," but the practical, rational among them said, "We've got to complete this launch. We have delayed it too long. We are beginning to look silly. We've got to get this one off." And so they did. Please acknowledge this tendency in yourselves and have as much compassion for them as you would for yourself. You have launched many things in your life against your intuition, and then said afterwards, "I knew

20

better. I really knew better." Just be grateful that all the world wasn't watching you on television!

So events moved forward on the earth plane. You were ready to move out, and this launching was supposed to be one of the first steps toward establishing a pattern to move in to, and eventually live in, outer space. But as I have told you before, no one is going to completely leave the sphere of this planet until there is harmlessness in their going. This is because right now there is harmfulness inherent in the actions of the people who are in charge of these missions. They do not understand the basic problems that could occur were you to begin moving this kind of energy farther and farther out into those areas of space. There is such a thing as an ongoing reaction. Let us suppose that you had established a colony out there, and one day something goes wrong and the colony is destroyed. In that explosion, in that action, a pattern of *re*action moves out. It creates an energy that begins to spark off other explosions. In a sense, my friends, it is a perfectly materialistic statement. Until you know how to go out into space in safety, then it isn't safe either for you or for space itself, because reactions do happen, reactions that continue on like a chain. When *you* are ready, when you exercise your capacity to intuitively know the things you do are safe, then, by all means, space will welcome you. But what do you think would happen at present if another country, let us say the Soviet Union, were to send a similar settlement out there? Then what would we have? Would we have two harmonious entities blending in peace, or would there be the fear that there might be a continuation of the hatred that has not been cleared up here? Would it not be possible for the feelings of mistrust which now exist between them to be sent into space as well?

Until harmony is here, it is not helpful to propagate the same kind of earth plane experience in a clean environment such as space. Space is clean, not filled at this time, but waiting. It is very much like a womb that is waiting for something wondrous to take shape in it. Space wants to become something greater. It wants to give birth to, and hold and embrace, a newness. And it is up to you to decide what kind of seed you wish to plant in this

21

womb. Not until your disharmonies are placed at rest here will you be qualified to go out and create new worlds. The Challenger is also a statement, my friends, of a desire from the other side of the veil, the unseen world. "Please stay and take care of things in your own homes. When you are in balance and harmony, then all of the Vastness will welcome you totally. We will invite you to come and share with us what you have and what you know. Until that time, it is safer for you, and it is safer for the whole Vastness, to keep the two areas separate."

Harmlessness is the basic issue, so let us now talk about it once again. I have often been asked how you would *know* what a harmless act is. The answer lies within. Please remember there is within you a power that knows what right action feels like. This power, when addressed by prayer, meditation, calling for help, or whatever seems appropriate at the moment, has the ability to respond to you with a very intimate, real, and creative awareness. When you are approaching any event, no matter how big or small, you can address the part of your psyche that knows the bold, vaster Plan, and has the delightful job of presenting you with the information it holds. It is the reservoir of your wonder, your beauty, your wisdom, and the culmination of all the things that have ever happened to you. It is the part of you that can be called the Knower, and its job is to wait until being called on, and then to tell you what it knows. And harmlessness it knows. As you have moved through all of your life cycles, you have accumulated an inner knowledge of what *harmlessness* is because you see so clearly what *harmfulness* is. You can take an event and ask yourselves if it is harmful or if it is not, and receive an answer. There is a deep, intuitive part of you that will say, "This is not for the good of all and I will not do it." The difficulty comes when your knowledge of harmlessness runs right up against the part of you that says, "I want what I want and I want it now." So, the answer is to quiet down your body long enough to hear that inner intuitive voice that speaks of harmlessness.

One reason you are asked to meditate and practice awareness is simply to fine tune this wonderful intuitive approach. Every time you have a decision to make, no matter how small, instead of going to the rational mind and asking what it thinks, go inside of yourself and ask, "How does it feel?" Do this a hundred times a day! You will know precisely what you should or should not eat, what job to take, what sentence to speak. You are not familiar with this inner dialogue because you are so busy acting out habitual patterns, belief systems, listening to others, following the mind, and on and on. Your own intuition can tell you how to stay safe. *You stay safe by going within and asking what is best for you.*

Another way of talking about harmlessness is to talk about Love. In its simplest form, Love could be described as an energy vortex which, when called upon, opens up the heart chakra to such an extent that you know what a loving action is. There is such a thing as a heart chakra and it can be opened. Love is that power which arises within you and moves out into the other parts of your awareness knowing what the loving thought is; which are the loving words; what is the loving action. The problem is you are always talking. When you wake up every morning, plant this statement deeply inside your awareness: *"As much as I am able this day, I will go within, ask and listen; and I am going to trust and risk by doing what I feel to be true. Thus, I will follow the response rather than the safety of my habituated patterns."*

When you start feeling there might indeed be some power that could change your present life totally, then we have the potential for surrender. When you admit that you don't know what to do or how to get over a heartache, or that you failed to be loving when you were angry, you open yourself to the possibility of receiving help from areas within you you didn't know existed. Surrender is simply saying, "I don't know. I am willing to give up all of what I think I know because it hasn't worked. And I ask that you teach me. I cannot teach myself, and I do not trust other people to teach me, because I find they are saying the same things I am." Out of this plea comes the dedication to put aside the old and become alert within yourself so new information can be made available. That is when you really begin to walk the Spiritual Path. You are stuck now because new information is not available to you, and it is not available because you are not listening to anything higher than your present awareness. When you talk

23

about wanting God-realization, you are talking about wanting to plug into the higher circuitry that is always humming around you. The dedication to listening to a higher awareness takes refinement. It takes a refinement of your habits, and it certainly takes a refinement in the way your body begins to respond to your listening process.

The job of the seeker is twofold: You have to ask and you have to listen. When you begin to listen with an expectation that there are exciting responses within you, and trust that you can follow them, you begin living a life you have never lived before. The side effect is that your body becomes healthier, you look younger, you become more alive, more extended, and more creative, all of the wondrous things you all want to be. But they are the side effects of listening and asking. You have no idea of the amount of help waiting to rush in when humility is present and the plea is made, "Teach me." Help surrounds you at all times. I spoke to you of the Comforter.[1] The Comforter is just one aspect of all of the multitudinous help that is always there. If you can begin by understanding *you have the ability to hear when you ask*, then you will listen. It becomes very simple. You know, the Path is not difficult. You simply have to experience the upliftment, joy, and awareness of that process.

The doorways are in you, and you open them by choosing to. At present, you have no idea of what is available to help you. You are not on this journey by yourself. If you think you are, I would give you a simple challenge—every day *give permission* to the energies that surround you to enter into your physical body, to transmute your old beliefs into new awareness, and to take the physical cells themselves and make them more radiant. Never in my experience have I found any human consciousness that reaches and asks, on a continuing basis, to not be answered. If you do not like your life and suspect that there may be something better, then ask for it!

The gift those high frequency powers can give you is their intuitive knowledge of how much your physical body can stand. Too much voltage in your body at one time will burn out your circuits. It is not your diet that gets in the way, it is your belief

24

systems that get in the way. You have accumulated an amazing amount of blockage, crystallization, and static through your belief systems, so when the energy starts moving into you, sometimes it feels painful. Sometimes you start to shake or twitch, or feel pain in different parts of your body. When you plug those higher frequencies in, you run right up against the old blockages of accumulated belief structures that act as a grid through which it is difficult for this energy to keep moving. So when you ask to be taught by these energies, they respond to you as you are ready to receive them, and you begin to make changes quietly, peacefully, and steadily. You can enhance your way by whatever you feel helps, but without this ongoing remembrance, without this constant dedication to greater awareness, very little can happen.

If you are living your life in order to increase your love and fullness of being, then everything turns around and is of value to you. It doesn't matter *what* you are doing. You can, in the midst of any action or event, be saying, "Teach me." You can keep your awareness so deeply placed within that you begin to respond to those higher circuits. You do not have to create the circuitry. Energy follows thought. When thought follows that circuitry, you begin to light up. In the end, it is a simple matter. The human psyche is used to doing fancy things, and that is the problem. It is difficult for you to be dedicated to calling for this kind of consciousness on a *daily, moment to moment* basis. When you want to become Enlightened, filled with Light, you have to get down past all separation, and rest in the knowing that you already are!

What do you think Home is? Home is that place within you which has total knowledge of the Source of All, and the moment you touch it, everything is made simple, delightful, and safe. It is your will, your desire, your willingness to blend with those higher vibrational frequencies which bring it about. You have created all of this. You will create Enlightenment if you will do one simple thing—remember that it is already there, already in you now! Claim the fact, and begin to ask yourself how you would act, what you would say if you were Enlightened? How would you treat people, how would you approach a given situation if you were

("act as if")

25

Enlightened? *What would you feel like?* Give yourself a chance.
Begin the process of *acting as if*, believing it is there and can be
brought forward, and trust you don't have to create it! Then
Enlightenment begins to be real for you. It is your belief system
that runs every moment of your life. I ask you to substitute for the
belief that you are a limited human being the reality that you are
an incredibly powerful vortex of amazing energy filled with life
and power that knows precisely what right action is on this earth
plane and anywhere else.

You are in a difficult position because your physical eyes
can't see the help surrounding you, and what the physical eyes
can't see is very hard for you to believe in. So the only hope left is
to open your inner eyes and see. Put aside the illusory idea that
you are not what you want to become. You all know exactly what
you want to be and how you want to move in this world. It is your
sorrow to think you don't know. But you do, and I am calling you
Home. As many moments as you can, go within and listen, call on
the help, feel it, and experience it. Hold to the simplicity of it and
you will begin to be filled with Light. You will be filled with Light
because the vibrational frequencies you will be resting in will enter
at a faster rate. I ask you, please, to consider the mastery we are
asking of you. The more of you who find yourselves filled with
Light and move out into the world with Light, the more the Light
on this planet will increase. So think about it. It is why you came.
It is the journey and the end. No more postponements. Please,
begin to know that you are Love and that you are Light.

---

[1]*The Comforter, page 165, "I Come As A Brother" by Bartholomew,
1986. High Mesa Press.*

Fourth Sharing
June 8, 1986
Taos, New Mexico

THE KINGDOM OF THE DEVAS

*Most workshops in Taos
are held in a small hexagonal
wooden building, on top of
the mesa west of town. From
this vantage point, one has
an unobstructed view of
Taos Mountain, considered
by many to be one of the
'power' mountains of the
world. In part, Bartholomew
chose this location because
of the mountain and
its energy.*

o then, good morning. As you have been often told, one of the hallmarks of the so-called New Age is to be an awakening in the human consciousness of the reality of other states of awareness. When aware of these states, man no longer feels the tremendous loneliness and isolation that is now a large part of his experience. In this New Age, as the barriers break down, man will begin to attune himself to other strong vortexes of energy whose delight it is to help, to make man aware that there is no such thing as separation, and there is indeed a wondrous, vast, universal tapestry that is being woven jointly by all the different parts of the One.

One of these vortexes has been prevalent, alive and conscious to the mystics of all ages, and comes through in the art of most great religions. I am, of course, referring to what, in the Christian tradition, is called the Angelic kingdom, and in the Indian tradition, the Devic kingdom. But whatever name you choose to use, it is helpful to know about this strand of consciousness because it can be used by you daily, wherever you are, to quicken the wondrous connection inside of you with other areas of vast consciousness and thereby alleviate your loneliness. I call this kingdom the kingdom of the Devas. I use the word Deva because of the sound Deva. The sound is so bold, so deep and clear, that it mirrors the inner sounds of the soul.

So, what exactly are Devas and of what importance are they to you? A Deva is an immense vortex of energy, grounded in the natural world, that can be found near mountain ranges, in the vast stretches of the sea, in the depths of great canyons, and are often a part of lakes and rivers. Many great cities of the world were founded in their vicinity because, although the human consciousness was not aware of it, man was pulled to these areas by the power of the Deva.

In the early days, the powers of the Deva were immense, and man was much closer to that energy. Many people could see them and a great many more could feel them. In those moments of knowing that such helpers did exist, man's heart became less afraid. If you were to observe a Deva of the mountain, for example, you would see a swirl of light and color, perhaps four times

29

the size of the mountain that it rests upon, extending down the slopes of the mountain and onto the plains below. These Devas hold themselves ready to receive energy from the Vastness, channeling this energy through their force fields and down to the land below.

If you were to ask a resident what the symbol of Taos, New Mexico is, you would almost always hear that it is the mountain. Now, as far as mountains go, Taos Mountain is alright, but many of you have seen higher, more impressive ones. There are even mountains taller and more impressive than this one located in the same mountain range. So why then, Taos Mountain? Why would this vast energy field choose to manifest in an area where so few people live? That is something I cannot really answer. All I know is that the Deva that rises above Taos Mountain likes it there. This Deva is very distinctive in its color. It is composed almost entirely of shades of blue and pink, sometimes falling off into purple and deeper blues. The Devas have different attributes, and these attributes carry with them different colors. In the case of the Taos Deva, its desire or attribute is to bring into you, on a cellular basis, two strands of consciousness, one represented by blue, the other by rose. Its job is to provide you with the opportunity to strengthen your will through the blue, and to soften your heart through the rose.

So how does one use the power of the Deva to help bring more love into your heart and more sweet will into your life? The answer is very simple: *energy follows thought*. Try sitting quietly in a mountainous area, or by a boiling river, or beside a thundering ocean. Then, if you can silence yourself even to a small degree and wait, you will find that there comes into your consciousness a feeling of other than human power. The power of a forest at night is quite different than the power of man. The feelings that come up as you sit beside the ocean and feel its thunder surround you are different from being in a crowded stadium. Sitting beside a river, watching and feeling its motion, you will find things begin to stir in you. It is this returning to the naturalness of things I am asking you to consider, and Devas are a part of this naturalness.

This can be experienced right here, right now. Let us do a

30

simple exercise that will illustrate what I mean. Sit quietly and still yourself. Imagine as best you can this wondrous Devic power, in whatever way it comes to you, and hold it deeply in your awareness. Feel the smallness of you and the vast largeness of it. See yourself seated before the Deva, looking up at it, or out at it, so that you will begin to take in the deeper rhythm that always exists when things are in their natural state. If there is an attribute, such as love, that you wish to manifest more strongly in your life, simply sit and ask that it be so. Dwell deeply on how it would feel to have that attribute active and alive in you. With your mind and awareness already joined to this much vaster power before you, you can come to feel the stirrings of what you are looking for.

This is real seeking, seating yourself before a vaster power and asking that it be joined with you, so that together you can overcome your feelings of isolation, of not being quite the way you wish you were. Turn your mind to this power, and you will realize that you are drawn to some part of the natural world, no matter where you are. You can be sitting in your living room in the midst of the largest city in the world and still feel this natural presence within you. So turn your mind toward the mountains or the sea or the river, feeling yourself, imagining yourself as being in that place, and simply ask for help. These Devas are not separate from any part of earth consciousness. It is in the attempting there is the finding, and without the attempt, you can be seated at the hem of the most powerful Deva in the world and miss it.

You have heard that the other strands of consciousness desire to awaken mankind to the possibility of your cohabitation of this planet. This is truly so. It is also interesting to be aware of the great delight that these vast energy fields have in being able to do the job that they came to do with man. So the New Age brings this opportunity yet again. "Ask and it shall be opened unto you"—an old truth as new and as old as all real truth is. Please take them seriously, my friends.

Q: Could you describe what the Deva of Taos Mountain looks like?

Try to envision a vortex of energy four times higher than the mountain itself, reaching out in both directions. We are talking about a very *large* Deva. The reason that psychics consider it female is because, as they see it, the Deva appears to have long, flowing hair. This, of course, they associate with the feminine. But if you look at the Indians of the local Tewa tribe, you will find that the men also have long, flowing hair. So the Taos Deva is simply a large shape, rounded at the top, and it rests partly above and partly in the mountain itself. The blue and the rose hues shimmer and glow, now dark, now light, constantly moving in brilliant patterns. The Deva is alive with power and energy. It is amazingly beautiful.

When it was time to pick a place for us to do our work, my only stipulation was that it would be a place where we had direct access to the mountain. It is my experience that the power of this Deva moves into your cellular structure to help you release the old and allow the new to take place. Those of you who live here or have lived here must have noted one very interesting thing. Nothing stays the same. Everything is in motion and many of you come simply for the total new beginning the Deva provides before moving you on to other places. It is important to realize that Devas have the power to draw you to an area and it has little to do with your conscious decisions. You get in your truck and start off for the coast and you break down in Taos, New Mexico. You can't get your axle fixed for six weeks, because that is the nature of the place. Before you know it, you have a house, a job, and a love affair, and there you are. Six years later you wonder what happened, so you pack up your truck again and head for the coast. It's a process.

Q: Speaking of the coast, are there Devas around large cities?

Devas do settle over large cities, but it takes a very different Deva to fill that role. The Deva around Los Angeles, for instance, would be described as much more 'masculine' in feeling. That's because Los Angeles is such an action area and people who go there need to get on with their lives in a very physical, material way. The whole state of California is interesting. There is one Deva around Los Angeles which also extends further south, and then almost abruptly another different one rises to the north, reaching up to San Francisco. Townships such as Santa Barbara belong to the San Francisco energy even though in proximity they are much closer to Los Angeles.

Devas differ as their responsibilities are different. If you were to go to Marseilles, which is another coastal city, you would see a Deva which is orange and dark brown in color. Its job is to transform the incredible negative energy that has been located in that area of the land for centuries. It does its best to take the energy into itself, lift it up, and transmute it to a higher frequency.

Q: I come from the Midwest and would like to know if there are Devas in the Minneapolis-St. Paul area.

There are lakes in the area you speak of. Some water Devas are drawn to the lakes and others are drawn to the sea. There are Devas of the ocean that are beautiful to behold, far vaster than anything you can imagine. Anywhere that you find quantities of water, you will find the Devic quality of nourishment.

Detroit is a city, for example, where much could go wrong because of all the financial difficulties and racial breakdowns, yet for such a large area it is extremely stable. Like Minneapolis-St. Paul, it has much greenery and many lakes. And both cities have attracted Devas of nourishment to help them.

Different areas attract different Devas with specific jobs. The Hawaiian Deva is very interesting. Being so close to water, it has the quality of nourishment, but at the same time it is also grounded on a volcano. Volcanos outpicture life in motion, so we are talking about growth. That mountain continues to build on itself and the Hawaiian Islands are creating an amazing, new consciousness. That area is the setting for one of the exciting experiments taking place on the earth plane today. Not only is the land building upon itself in Hawaii, but the people, should they be so disposed, will be able to develop a newer consciousness. It is not an old and stuffy place, so therefore the new has an opportunity to take shape and form much more readily there. Hawaii is a migrating place and has always been such. The birds migrate through it, the fish come and go, everything is in movement. So, we'll see. Because it is a melting pot for many different cultures, it has as a basis the exciting potential of bringing real brotherhood. It's an experiment and it is delightful.

Q: I have been living in Jerusalem for the past year and wonder if you would you comment on the energy in Israel.

When we talk about Israel, we have to drop away much of the country and talk about Jerusalem. If you look at the mountains around that area, you will see that they are stark, they are strong, they are enduring. The Deva reflects those qualities, and the colors there are often the browns and deep yellows. The Deva of Jerusalem stands at a crossroads in that part of the world and the job is always the same—how best to stabilize the minds and hearts of the people. The land itself attracts, because it holds a deep—and I hope this word isn't offensive—religion. In Jerusalem we are talking about a need to bring order into the hearts and minds of man. And one way to bring about a deep, internal order is through the discipline of religion. So, Jerusalem is a pivotal area, useful for bringing this harmony about. And the job is incredibly difficult because there are so many diverse peoples creating much separation. But when you want to get your life 'in order' in the deepest sense, go to Jerusalem.

Jerusalem is very close to the Deva because it stays close to the earth, still holding to the Mother, because that is where the power comes from. Great vertical cities, such as New York, have difficulty because they have lost contact with the earth. Tempting as it is, don't live in the top of a high-rise. Stay down close to the Mother and let your consciousness rise up. When you live high up in a tall building, your body is between two worlds. It is too far from Mother Earth to feel her groundedness, and it is a false rising up because it is not your consciousness that goes up in the elevator but your body. So you find yourself somewhat disconnected. If you go that same vertical distance on a mountain, you will retain the groundedness because Mother Earth is there with you. Tall buildings have a tendency to sway. They have very little real centered consciousness. And if things get too rough, they will snap. No matter what the steel girders say to you, they will snap.

Q: You have spoken about Israel. Would you also speak of the Middle East? There is so much confusion and turmoil in that area that I wonder if many different Devas are there.

This answer may sound as though it is a political statement, but I assure you that I speak from a level far deeper than that. The Middle East is trying to make one statement to mankind, and they are saying it with a loud, militant voice. But nevertheless, what they are saying should be heard. They are asking to join, with equality, the brotherhood of man. They do not want to be the poor, outcast, uneducated, unappreciated part of mankind. They want to stand as equals to their brothers and sisters wherever they might find themselves. They have been asking for equality for centuries and have never had it bestowed. There has always been an arrogance on the part of the educated, of the sophisticated, of those who have moved into the intellectual realm, and, in comparison, they look like children. Because they are looked upon as children, they are acting like children, but they are making a statement that must be heard: *There is no separation between us!* They will fight and die until they are heard and admitted as equals to the Oneness of man on this planet. They represent the fearful part in everyone, the part that wants to get its needs met and cries out in that desire, and then starts to destroy until it gets what it needs. That consciousness is not separate from any one of you. There is a part of you that fights in the hills of Beruit, that starves in the mountains of Afghanistan. It's all One. Their cry is simple. They want integration on a vaster scale. The Deva's job there is to do what it can to cool the hearts and minds of its people because they are angry. With all due respect, they have something to be angry about.

Q: Could you also speak of Africa and Central America?

They are very different. Africa has always had quite a responsibility. Africa carries the shadow of the planet. If you ever think in terms of archetypes, you will realize that different parts of the globe carry different parts of the archetypes. And Africa, the dark continent, the Black, is the shadow. They are simply saying, on a planetary scale, that it is time to pay attention to the shadow. They have been asleep, but they are waking up. And as the shadow is waking up in you, as the shadow is starting to hum and sing and start playing with your consciousness here, so it will outpicture in Africa. Whatever the end for that area, the symbol is very clear. It is time for the shadows to awaken, to come out into the sunlight and begin to take charge of their own lives. I ask you as well to pay attention to your shadows and get them integrated as a part of your system, instead of trying to subjugate and control them.

Although nothing is absolutely guaranteed, chances are excellent that the struggle taking place in Africa will end up with the Blacks winning their freedom. And when they do, they will then have to struggle with their own shadows. Once the victory is over and they have control of their own country, *their* shadows will come out. Will they then play out the same apartheid roles with their brothers and subjugate them into different classes or will they integrate their own shadow? As they face this dilemma, they will move very definitely into the twentieth century. Any time you integrate any part of your shadow, you are helping to integrate it for the rest of the world. The hope for Africa would be that they do not throw away the wondrous things that make them so unique, and that they refuse to copy the White man's pattern.

When we come to your wonderful American neighbors to the south, we have a different situation. If you want to talk about the place on the planet that has heart, we have to talk about South and Central America. It is the sense of having twelve children that you can barely feed, and a stranger knocks at your door. Now you have thirteen mouths to feed and you do it. These are not people who bar their doors to a wanderer. This is the wonderful abundant *heart* area of the planet. So we have the intellect to the North and the heart in the South. What is needed is a road between the two. There is no question that you, as a nation, could have helped those countries to the south if the road between your nation's mind and heart had been open in the psychic sense. When heart and mind are joined, you will find a mutual nourishment moving both ways. But now, because the mind is in control, the roadways between those two parts of consciousness are closed off.

The beauty is that the southern heart goes on beating. Per-

36

haps you noticed the amazing struggles of the Mexican people to help when Mexico City had a recent earthquake disaster. Relentlessly, hour after hour, day after day, they worked, often to save a single life. So the heart is alive and mostly well. It's just that it is hungry in the physical sense, therefore it slows down its rate a bit. As the balance comes and the mind and the heart of the planet start moving in unison, there is all hope. If you can view these things as symbolic and then do what you can in your own consciousness to unite your mind and heart, you will see that these planetary divisions need not exist. Do your job within your own being with those unifying ideas in mind, and things will begin to lighten.

Q: In speaking of the symbology of countries, would you talk briefly about China?

Well, you know when you think about China, you have to think big. Very, very big. However, you really cannot separate China from her neighbor, Japan. They have separated themselves with a small body of water, but in reality, that whole part of the createdness stands for inventiveness. Those peoples hold the intuitively inventive capacity. They come up with the new art forms, not in the intellectual, but in the intuitive sense. That part of the planet is the place that produces a new way to fire a pot that will increase its beauty a thousandfold. They are the artists. They have the soul of the artists and in this the two countries are not separate. They are the artistic, the creative, the inventive, that wonderful part of mankind that says, "How beautiful we are! How beautiful you are!"

In China, it is a tremendous help to have many people because, as an agrarian nation, they will not move into the 'mental life' of the city. Thus they can keep their natural intuitive awareness. Many intuitive things are being born in those small villages that are expressed as art forms. Just look at their kites, for instance. Think of it. In America, you have kites with pretty basic shapes that you put a string on and it goes up and down. They are very geometric, very mental. But this is not what you have in China. And this is not what you have in Japan. There, you have kites so large that children can fly over the rice paddies in them.

We are talking about an incredibly creative, artistic soul coming through in myriad forms.

So the Devas, which is where we started, stand as reminders. Please understand that all of the energy a Deva pours out into the world can be felt in a very definite way. It goes into and becomes a part of the cellular structure of those who dwell with it. Do not forget that you, as a wandering, incarnating being of consciousness, have recorded in your cellular structure in one incarnation or another, *all* of the different Devic energies. You would not bother to listen to me prattle about Godly things if you had not recorded within you the memory that God Is! And the Devas help to remind you. They remember and delight in the job of passing such memory on.

The question which arises with consciousness is, "Given that I am a human, how can I also feel my Divinity, in the midst of that humanness?" That is your one real question, asked a million different ways. I see the answer as simple—turn within, *feel* yourself present in your body, and relax into your inner space. The answers that you seek are recorded in the cells of your being. When you want to know something, *ask your Self*. When you want to know how to rise to the heights of your consciousness, *ask your Self*. You are the Way to the Truth and the Light!

Fifth Sharing
June 22, 1986
Albuquerque, New Mexico

THE ENDLESS SKY

I was asked why, when there are limited workshop opportunities in Taos, we selected as one of our topics Vipassana.[1] It appears to be a very strange word, and many people coming out of the Christian tradition find it suspect. I am not going to talk about the subject, but about what Vipassana has to do with you, your growth, your possible realization, and your freedom.

[1]*Vipassana is mindfulness meditation. It is concerned with following the panorama of what is going on with impartial attention. Sitting begins with the simplest object of meditation, which is the breath. Awareness is placed on the rise and fall of the breath, and all sensations, thoughts, sounds, or sights in the body are impartially noted. Attention is always returned to the breath.*

There are many voices the Divine speaks with on your planet. And one should not, in my estimation, fall into judgment of which is best, or which is better. It is simply a matter of which one resounds most deeply within your physical being, lights up your mind, gives you hope for clarity and a possible awakening, and a way to fly Home. So if this information today strikes a chord in you, it will be because you realize what it is Vipassana can do. The basic essential truth of the teaching is simply this: *You have made a mis-identification.* You have identified yourself with the clouds that pass to and fro in the sky, but you are, indeed, the sky itself. The clouds, according to this tradition, are all of the points of duality—love and hate, war and peace, rich and poor, etc. You know the dualities well, and these are the clouds that pass through you, about you, and hopefully out of you and on their way.

What would be a way to perceive this old truth in a new way? Every thought and action that you have accumulated on the earth plane, as a human consciousness, still remains present. All of the mass events, and all of your own personal events, go together to form a vortex of power and energy that keeps revolving around the globe. There is such a thing as energy in motion, and this energy continues to circle your globe, which is why you can say there is such a thing as 'world karma,' or a 'world idea.' Since the beginning of man's journey here, all of these positive and negative ideas and actions, and all of the rules and regulations that have come down through the ages, can still be found here.

When you begin any spiritual path, you also begin to magnetize your own energy field. In doing this, you draw to you all of the accumulated truths and untruths associated with that particular system. Unfortunately there is no way to filter out the untruth and just leave the truth shining by itself. Energy is energy and you cannot put rules on it. So when you begin an 'ascent to the mountain peak' through a certain tradition, you magnetize yourself in line with that particular consciousness. People follow different traditions and become aware and awake in different ways. So the job is how to love past all of the clouds and to simply love from the Vast Sky.

When we begin to talk about the truths in Vipassana, or the Zen tradition, what are we speaking about? Those monks came to know, through a very austere method of meditation, that there was no personal 'I' moving through lifetime after lifetime, accumulating karma, etc. What they found instead was amazing. If they sat quietly with enough determination, yet ease, they found the dualities would rise and, if they persevered in their quiet watching and nonjudgmental attention, *they would also leave.* Hatred, anger, resentment, all of the emotions, arose in their consciousness. But, by the quiet contemplation of them, making no judgment about what they felt, they realized those emotions simply drifted out of their awareness and, lo and behold, something else arose.

The monks sat there long enough to see it was very difficult to only allow light and love into their awareness, because right on the back of those wonderful feelings almost always would come what you would call negative ones. As the weeks, months, and years drifted by, they came to the knowledge that they had misunderstood something very simple. They had mistaken themselves, the sense of who they were, for those emotions, for the passing clouds. They were always trying to decide, "Is this a cloud I should allow to enter me? Is this a good cloud? Is this a bad cloud? Is this cloud right? Is this cloud wrong?" The struggle, as they tried to sift through these different layers, showed them that the rules they had been trying to follow were of no help. Some came from the Indian tradition, which is interesting, but rather complicated because of the rules one must follow.

So these first monks had quite a job of it, trying to follow the rules, be quiet, and become enlightened. They struggled to rid themselves of all negative thought and feeling and enter into a state of bliss. They found they simplified their lives to such a point that all they did was eat very little and meditate all day. Therefore there wasn't much opportunity for negativity to come rolling in. Make no mistake, these were real warriors of their time, but nevertheless, they were finding there was something essentially missing when they left their peaceful caves of isolation. Back into the township they would go to buy their bag of rice, and, lo and behold, they might get jostled or a shopkeeper might give them the wrong change or tell them to leave because they smelled so bad. And then, unless they had truly reached a clear state of awareness, up would arise the duality and away they would go again!

Is it possible to keep the negative away from your consciousness? Is there anything you can do to so purify youself that you will never have a negative thought, never perform a negative act, but always think in loving kindness? I am sure you have tried to, because it is part of the Path. But I ask you also to be honest about your own success. How much have you succeeded?

You are wonderful and amazing people and I see in your consciousness a tremendous amount of true striving, a desire to awaken, to have loving kindness and Christ Consciousness in your hearts. So we have to ask if you do not because you are not good enough or don't try hard enough? I would like to suggest something slightly different for you to consider. Is it not possible the goal is to become aware of the same thing those courageous monks observed so long ago, that you, through objective observation of your own life, can come to see you are *something through which the positive and negative poles of this planet move*? They come to you! Is it possible that all of the energy which has been revolving in its own pattern around the globe comes down to you, enters you, and exits? And the job, perhaps, is not to keep the doors shut, to keep the negative out, because in so doing you also deny the positive?

There is a doorway to awareness in each individual and it is either open or closed. When it is open, anything moving through, around, or in this planet will be welcome to move through you and out. Allow it to happen. Practice and you will begin to develop the feeling of *space* within you. This is why we have Vipassana workshops, to force twenty-four strong warriors to sit and watch, to walk and watch, to eat and watch. To simply give them an opportunity to begin to *feel* that space and to understand what inner space really means.

On a physiological level, you know there is a lot of space within and around the cells. You are filled with space. It is that space which reflects the knowingness of the Vast Sky. It is exciting to watch the thunderclouds as well as the beautiful clouds move through you, because you will realize *experientially*, not mentally, that something is present other than the motion of the clouds. Do not trap yourself by trying to categorize that feeling. Do not label that 'otherness' God. There is always something the mind would like to grab onto and feed back to you, so you can worship it and be safe. The moment you worship something else, duality is present. Worship implies two, that which is being worshipped and the one doing the worshipping. The moment that separated thought arises in your consciousness, you are off the track.

This other feeling, this knowingness, this awareness that begins to arise in you, if consistently paid attention to, will tell you directly, all you need to know. The way to the Divine often is through patience, a quality that is very difficult on a busy planet where people are always *doing* something. The reason we keep maintaining that some kind of dedicated practice of meditation is helpful is because of the following. Inside the space of your body and inside the space of your psyche, there is a power and awareness that, *when paid attention to*, begins to calm down your entire system, take the edge off your pain, and stimulate a sweet feeling within you. It is called 'belief.' Until the moment you *feel* the Divine, you are only someone *trying* to believe. The moment that you, with awareness, let this spatial quality move within you, you will experience the hope that says, "It is true. God exists and exists in me." Do this enough and God becomes a reality because the space is so much vaster than the concept in your mind.

It is at this point, confusion will arise. All of the concepts and ingrained beliefs about what God wants and requires from you before He will love and accept you crash up against the reality that *GOD IS!* Now that you *believe*, you also experience *fear*. What if it isn't true? What if God isn't really there? In that moment, the fear becomes so overwhelming that many people turn to religion in the hope the rules will make them safe.

When this duality faces you, what do you do? You do the very same thing you have been doing to get to the point of God-awareness in the first place. You become very, very big, because you are holding in your consciousness two things: God and fear.

44

The immensity of God and the immensity of your fear. At that point, many people start to wobble. Just stay with it. Laugh if you can, watch the fear, feel the God-Self, feel the feeling of the fear you have just found you cannot possibly get rid of. So, at that point, you have to become very big to encompass both.

When I had this experience, it fit into the category of what you call 'the dark night of the soul.' I decided that the only way out was to stop struggling and allow the forces of 'dark and light' to fight it out themselves. I finally realized I could not do it. With my limited understanding, I had no hope of ever settling anything between these two amazing powers which were struggling for victory in my consciousness. Every time I would move toward one, the other seemed to get larger and larger, and the first one farther and farther away. So then, being a warrior, I would try the other side, hoping to reverse the process. You see, I was trying to trick God into deciding for me. This went on for what seemed a long time.

What was the outcome? I was sitting there filled with depression, then light, then depression, then light, wobbling! Back and forth. But then one day, opening my eyes and looking out, I saw an endless sky, and it happened at that moment the sun was setting. I saw reflected on one of the cloud clusters an immense golden light, representative, I thought, of the golden side of me. Equally powerful, a dark, gloomy, thundering black cloud was present next to it. I sat there watching, even to the end projecting all of who I was out there. And as I watched, both of the clouds began to disappear. In those moments, as I kept staring at both of them disappearing, I saw the dark evening sky *coming through them.* Then suddenly, as in the great Zen stories, a brick dropped and Enlightenment happened. In my case, the clouds disappeared and awareness was present.

I tell you this because I believe with all of my Being you can follow this same pattern in your present life. Begin to experience *yourself* as the Vast Sky and observe moving through you the endless clouds. When you are paying attention to your thoughts, you will see clearly they rise and fall, and there is a space between them. You are *not* one continuous, chattering mind. When you

45

look for the spaces, when you begin to identify with the Sky and abandon what I might call—I hope with humor—the neurotic tendency to pay attention to the clouds, you will begin to get a sense of how very vast your consciousness is.

You do not have to destroy every cloud to see the sky. All you have to do is keep remembering you are the Sky. And you can do that because it is true! Since you have misidentified yourself in the first place, you have the capability of reidentifying yourself. You thought yourself into this and you can think yourself out of it! You are not all of the polarities you think you are. You do possess them in some measure, but they move through you. You will never, ever clean up your clouds sufficiently, my friends. There will always be a little dark one that you can't quite get at. There will always be one somewhere that you can't quite reach.

So, what again to do? Just continue what you are doing, but with a slight shift. Start feeling yourself as the Vast Sky, and let the clouds do what they do. The winds of karma do blow, and I advise you not to try to get them to blow the way you want them to. Karma is an energy form that pushes the clouds around in your particular sky. All you have to do, my friends, is start reidentifying yourself, dropping the belief that you are a limited, polarity-pulled consciousness, and commit deeply to being the Vastness that you are. Any other concept of yourself is a limitation.

You are not the actions you perform any more than the figures on a screen projected in a movie are the screen itself. The most incredible holocaust can be projected onto that screen and it will remain unchanged. The most wondrously uplifting statement can be shown on the screen and it still remains unchanged. *You are changeless. You are eternal.* And the rest is *your* illusion. Concentrate on who you really are and you will know! There is no other solution, my friends. You cannot clean up your clouds, and you don't need to.

Sixth Sharing
September 28, 1986
Albuquerque, New Mexico

SAFETY IS AN INSIDE JOB

In the closing months of 1986, I became aware of a certain 'difference' in the way the monthly Albuquerque sessions were feeling. The information seemed 'further out there,' and in order to work with it, I had to 'stretch.' This meant relaxing into a vaster, fuller area of consciousness than I ever had before. It meant 'letting go' on a deeper level—trusting the Energy would carry me firmly enough so I could give word-form to what I was experiencing. We decided to include these transcripts because we honestly feel they represent new information. We seem to be moving into totally new areas, and we wanted to share this newness with you.

Mary Margaret Moore

oday, I would like to help you envision exactly what happens to your physical body when energy moves into it. Then let us discuss how to incorporate this re-enlivened vision into a way that will enable you to live your life with power.

It is very clear to me the basic issue before you here is how to feel safe in an unsafe world. Until you do, the *cells* of your body will not relax, and until the cells relax, you will not allow what you call 'enlightenment' to pour forth. This state of Light consciousness you seek is *within you*. It is all here and as much here in this moment, in this place, and in you as it ever will be. You can never go anywhere else and find more God. And even if you feel this as a concept rather than a reality, you must find a way to relax the cells of your body so they can give up the treasure that lies within them.

You come from a water-based planet. As this planet is made up mostly of water, it is also true that the physical body is composed mostly of water. So then, we can say that you are a water-based consciousness. It is *water* which has the capacity to retain that which you seek. The Divine has always been bombarding you with the Power to make your life clearer, truer, and more of what you want. And it is within the water of the cells that this incredible force field lodges itself. The very cells of your body are 'accumulators,' and they are accumulating that which you need, and that which is absolutely essential to your well-being.

Humans are constantly assessing the area around them, asking, "How safe am I in this situation?" When you are with a person who considers you to be less than he or she is in any way, your being knows this. Your whole cellular structure contracts because you know this person has judged you and therefore is not safe. And when you do not feel safe, you are not going to open up your being because fear is present. You are afraid of ridicule, afraid of judgment, afraid of being found to be less, and none of those emotional states are safe.

Yet, you can go to a lake in the midst of a mountain, by yourself, and all of a sudden find yourself transfixed. In a state of expansion, you feel the sky, the trees, the water. You know there is a God. YOU KNOW IT. And what is the difference? Here you

49

feel safe. Your energy goes out and embraces the environment and as far as you can see you feel acceptance. There is no fear. In those moments of acceptance, the cells relax, and out of that relaxation arises what you call enlightenment. *Your cells give up their essence of Light*. This is not a mental process. Your entire body participates. Every part of you is alive and expanded in a new way, and as you fill yourself with this feeling, you thank God that the Divine and you co-exist.

So if the expansion which you seek can only be found in places that feel safe, how then to live your life? For you must have come to the startling realization that the world does not appear safe! And what in this unsafe world are you most afraid of? It is simple to find out. Stop for a moment and visualize yourself completely alone on a black, deserted plateau. What is it you are afraid will come out of the dark? Most of the time you are afraid of each other. And that is because you have spent lifetimes making *each other* afraid. So *you* have created an unsafe world.

But the problem still remains. So let us go back to the basic cellular structure. Your cells have two choices—they can either expand or contract. When the cells expand, they release the Divine energy stored in them and you find yourself to be in a state of expansion. And when you are expanded and extended into your life, you feel alive no matter what is going on around you. But many of you have withdrawn your energy from the world. Even though you are in it, you are not of it. You are not participating in life, therefore you do not feel enlivened. You have contracted out of pain and fear of pain. When the cells of your body are contracted, none of that stored Divine energy is available in your life. Retreating from the world because you experience pain does not feel good. In the literal sense, when your heart is not open, it aches. So if you have an aching heart, it is not because somebody hurt you. It is because you have retreated into yourself and your cells are now contracted and producing physical pain. An aching heart is a physical phenomena. It is not a psychic one. It is pressure on the body itself, and you feel as if your heart is breaking.

Many of your lives are concerned with what you have chosen to call the New Age. And one way of talking about the New Age

50

is to say you will be creating new building blocks of consciousness. All things are created out of the same substance. We could call this substance God, the Source, the All, the One, or whatever you choose. This Source creates vast numbers of different levels of consciousness, and a new level of consciousness for the earth plane is in the process of being created at this time. New, deeper awarenesses are used as the building blocks of this consciousness. And the cells of your body can be given a new message through the use of them. They can be used as a child uses toy blocks. What you build is up to you. Many of you are starting to *experience* the reality of your mind creating your world. So it is time to create a new cellular message. In the past, your cells have had the job of paying attention outwardly to all kinds of psychic and physical movement in order to keep you safe. That is an old message, and it came out of a time that is no longer appropriate. So the cells need to hear a new message, and in the hearing, they will take on the responsibility of extending out into an area where they do not need to be afraid.

Safety does not lie in contraction. Something has gone awry because you have *believed* that *contraction* could make you safe. Now practice the opposite. Start believing that it is *expansion* that will make you safe, and then be the observer. You can find a hundred ways to expand every day. Just try it. In the midst of something that looks frightening, start expanding with your breath. The natural act of filling your lungs with air will straighten your spine and extend your chest. Then you will be 'leading with the heart.' And the heart is where you feel the love. If love is 'the way,' how can you possibly think that giving love under any circumstance could hurt you? It is the love moving out of your cellular body that keeps you safe. When you choose extension, *your love has the ability to change your environment*! You may find the feeling of extension so blissful in itself that you do it, not to change your environment, but because *it feels good*. You are not going to do something consistently on a conscious level that feels bad. You contract because you haven't been *conscious* of your contraction.

Start paying attention. When your husband or wife walks in and says, "Dear, I have something to tell you," do you expand or contract? When your child hasn't come home and it's three in the morning, do you feel like expanding or contracting? Sitting in a traffic jam, do you feel expansion or contraction? Test this theory, be aware of the differences, and then *choose a new response.* God is not going to rush in and fill you. God is already totally present in you. Safety is an inside job. It is in those moments that you choose to relax and expand that you will know that you are filled with Light. You will literally see it in your mind and feel it in your heart. Your body will sing in a way that it never has before, and you will know you are safe.

One way to help change the old belief structure that says contraction equals safety is to create a safe space in your environment in which to feel the new. People experience God in places of worship because they have historically been physical places of safety. Those of you who meditate create 'safety zones.' Setting the meditation time and place produces a feeling of safety, so when you sit down, your cells can relax and open. Many of you also feel safe in your deep, natural sleep state. You allow yourselves to then relax, and in so doing fly to amazing places of wonder, strength, and remembrance. So find a place that is yours, light the candles, burn the incense, smell the flowers, and *relax.* The message of safety has got to come on a cellular level. If you do not practice this on a consistent basis, your cells are going to obey the unconscious directive which tells them to close down.

So let us end where we began. When you came out of the sea and moved to the land, your cells still contained the water of the sea. That cellular water is the part of you that is the collector of the Light. You do not have to be in any particular place to be a collector because the Divine can't miss you. Since there is no way you can hide, everyone is equally a collector. Now is the time to begin using that which you have collected to make you safe. It is your responsibility, my friends, to maximize those things that make you feel safe and minimize the ones that don't. If there are situations you cannot change, extend into them anyway! You will not die! Every time you let go and extend into a difficult circumstance, what always comes forward is love, and when love moves out into your world, at that moment you are so much safer than you were the moment before. You have two choices. Extension brings love and contraction adds to your fear. Which will you choose? It's all a matter of practice.

The advantage of having incarnated at this time is that the *frequency* of Divine Power moving across the earth has greatly increased. The *amount* of Divine Power cannot vary. But now, with the increase of frequency, you can expand and caress It or you can contract and reject It. Every time you choose extension, no matter what the circumstances, you will be filled with Divine Power which says, "God's in It's Heaven and all's right with *my* world."

Seventh Sharing
February 22, 1987
Albuquerque, New Mexico

DIVINE RELATIONSHIP

This morning, I would like to talk once again about a different model of consciousness. Used with awareness, it can help you come to a point of inner clarity, wisdom, and totality. To do this, we will speak about a realm difficult for most of you, which is that of relationships. I believe it is difficult because you do not really know what is going on when you are trying to relate. So then, I think a discussion of this type would be relevant today.

he model of relationship I am talking about is not new at all, but when brought forward now, is new to your present awareness. The first thing to bring forward in your consciousness is the awareness that you are a vortex of energy, constantly in motion, propelled by events, sounds, colors, everything you have sensory contact with. You can begin to feel those energies, if you choose to do so. This individual expanding, contracting, vortex of power is fed by springs and streams unknown to you, and when two or more of you are present, we have a combination of energy fields in motion. This greatly increases the potentiality as well as the complexity of what I wish to dwell on.

One analogy to use in talking about who and what you are is to visualize yourself as a cup or chalice, which is rather how you appear psychically. The cup has a wonderful openness which is filled with a mixture of moving energy. Other people present themselves in exactly the same way, but different essences have difficulty intermingling with each other because of the walls of the chalice. If, even for a few moments, you could really touch, taste, and feel the elixir of wonder in any other cup, the experience would be so revealing there would be no chance of further separation.

What then is the major ingredient in the chalice wall that keeps the inner elixir from being accessible? My friends, it will not be a surprise when I tell you it is guilt. *Guilt*! In the beginning of your earth plane experience, you had one rule to guide you and we have talked about it before. It is still the guiding rule—*to live harmlessly*, to live as best you can so you harm no one. And out of the original ability to feel and touch what was harmless, you were able, in those moments, to see each other with clarity. But, as things happened, various rules and regulations, which you now call religions, began to rise, and there arose also different and various laws. You accumulated a long array of very specific things to juggle in order to be 'good enough' —certain kinds of food, certain kinds of behavior, thoughts, actions, emotions, and on and on. So when you were attempting to connect with the God-Self, obstacles were felt, guilt entered, and you became afraid to open up the

55

channel to what you call the Divine High Self of who you are.

The moment guilt came into your awareness, there arose a fear of God. I have told you before, many of you are *afraid* of God, because the God *you* have created is such a fearful one. This image is simply a projection from the minds of man and not at all true. Nevertheless, there remains deeply embedded in the cellular remembrance of your whole beingness the idea that, if you don't measure up, you are going to be destroyed, or at best punished by being sent to some dark area, which sounds far worse than being totally annihilated. This middle ground is where you go if you are sort of bad or sort of good, and there you stay until sometime, somehow, something magical happens and you are no longer in such jeopardy and they release you to something else.

My friends, I am trying to lighten up a very frightening view of life and God that is embedded in your psyches. Many of you are no longer actively trying to open up your channel to the Divine. There is the fear that if you do, you will find that you are not loved. Please imagine how it must feel inside your consciousness to know there is an almighty, wondrous God, and at the same time know that It could be angry at you. Understand, there is a deep part of you that responds to this belief with fear. Now, given the dilemma, what is the solution?

There are a great many human beings on this earth plane and you have been told that the greatest friends you have are each other. So we go back to our diagram of relationship. Each time you open your mouth, or use your eyes or your body to connect and make contact with others, you are doing one of two things: *adding to the fear and guilt or adding to the joy and light in the other person and in the world.* You do not help yourself by dwelling on your own darkness. That is only a way you keep a negative image of yourself before your consciousness. What you have to learn is the necessity of sending clear messages about what you truly want to the Deep Self. Your Deep Self is also an energy vortex, and it is waiting to be quickened in whatever way you choose. It waits in eternal patience for you to turn to it on your own behalf, and when you ask, you must be specific. What exactly is it that you want? Do you want to find out who you *really are*, what reality *really is?* Then ask the Deep Self to reveal those Truths!

The lower, separated self believes you are a linear, limited, often ill, often unhappy, poor little worm, walking over the globe in a chaotic pattern, going you know not where, doing you know not what. The lower self pleads with God to be delivered from this life as soon as possible. Each time you open your mouth, you either increase everyone else's belief in their own lower self, or their belief in Truth. So, the greatest help you can give to yourself and others is to constantly remember that you are Light, you are Love, you are exploding creation, limitless and harmless. *You are all the things you have yearned so much to be.* You could not yearn to be those things if you were not *already them.* Please understand this. What you want to do is build within the wonderful vessel of your beingness the power of your own remembered, unspecified Love, the feeling of Love in motion within you, until you can taste the elixir and feel that it is possible to truly Love all of the createdness. And it comes out of starting *now.*

There is nothing magical about enlightenment. Nothing! The Light is in there, waiting to explode. The Light is out here, waiting to join with what's inside. We have discussed the only thing that stands between them, which is the chalice itself. The inside is filled, and the outside is equally filled, but it is the structure of guilt between that keeps the Light from enlivening you so that *It lives you* in a way that is totally beyond speech. It brings a quickening, an aliveness to the totality of everything you do, and it is worth everything to achieve. Begin this day to build your internal power so that you can literally burst through the barrier of guilt and allow yourself to re-experience the connection with the One God.

It is not that you have to be 'good,' just stop believing you are 'bad.' You can change that belief by experiencing the *wonder of who you are.* If you begin every day to sit with your own energy field, remembering the things you truly are, and *dare* to tell yourself they are true, *you will quicken the awareness of the Source so strongly that you will feel It.* I mean feel It with a tangibility that will answer all your questions.

There is a new term I have heard come up with people to

describe relationships that aren't working. The word is 'dysfunction-al' and the phrase is 'coming from a dysfunctional family.' Well, the news is that you all come from dysfunctional families. And I will tell you why. Because any family who doesn't know who *they* are will provide you with a picture of who you are that is *not* true. They, out of their own illusory confusion, have projected onto you the same confusion. All families are dysfunctional. You can split it up into any degree of dysfunction you wish, but I see it only one way. You either know who you are or you don't!

Until the moment you break through the web of guilt, you will not be functioning in some way or another. I mean this with all of the Love that I have. The *only* thing keeping you from totally knowing who you are is the grid work of your *own belief* of who you are. I will tell you again, you are *total Love*, *total Divine Power—activated*! You are a symphony of color and sound past the wildest imaginings of your physical body, which illuminates your mind and heart. *That is who you are.* Anything short of that is a lie, and I beg you to stop perpetuating the lie.

As your birthright, you have the ability to break through the blockage of guilt and experience yourself totally. You cannot shovel out the darkness. It will take forever. The best way to fill a room with light is to open the window. Your job is to do it all the time. When someone is saying something to you that is born in illusion, instead of participating in the lie, become very still within, remember and activate the memory of that which you seek. In the face of any of your own dismal thoughts, stop and remember you are part of the Divine. Do not try to be perfect. You are never going to make it. Do you understand? You cannot be perfect in a physical body because the physical body sees things as separated. But out of the growing power within, you can explode out of the dream of separation into the reality of Oneness.

In a relationship, what you see of a person most of the time is an illusory reflection shining back off the chalice itself, prevent-ing you from seeing into the depths. You are always in relation-ship, and I am not talking about love affairs. They are only a small part of relationship. I am talking about life, about relating to every-one you see. Every moment of your day, when you are in the presence of another, you have the opportunity to increase your movement toward enlightenment. If you decide to increase your ability to experience Godness within, when you look at the other person, you *must* remember that they too are God. What happens then is you increase your vibration and release 'God' energy into the atmosphere around you. In that instant, you activate in some measure the other person's own remembrance. You are the mirrors, each for the other. And when you remember that as much as you can, you will be incredibly helpful to each other.

That is why an Enlightened One is helpful. They look at you and start to laugh. "Do you really believe that's who you are? Do you really believe in those limitations? Do you really?" If they don't, if you have a teacher who scolds you, get a new teacher! Because anyone who does not see that you are God manifesting hasn't had the full experience of enlightenment. So don't be scolded. You have been scolded enough, and you scold *yourselves* endlessly. If you want a real teacher, please get someone who knows you are playing a game and will reflect back who you truly are.

What you are being asked to give up is what the 'lower' self loves best, which is the desire to be right. This illusory self adores being right, because being right also means being all-right. And being alright makes you feel, for a moment, more secure. So be watchful, because the only question that ever arises when you are dealing with the Vast Self is this, "Are you willing to lay down everything else in order to reflect the truth?" And the truth is the reality of the Light, Love, Power, and total amazement of who you all really are.

Every time you help your brother or sister to see this, you have helped yourself. It cannot be other than that, and so I ask those of you who really want to experience Light in the mind and in the heart to begin in this simple way. *Remember*! Whatever else is going on, don't forget! And each time you remember, trust that you are building the energy in your body. There is nothing new outside of you that isn't inside, and you build that energy by your own sweet remembrance. Do it now, or do it later, but you *will* do it, because a deep part of the human consciousness has an incredible longing to be Free. I often use the word Freedom because it best reflects the feeling of breaking loose from the chains of illusion and soaring into the Vastness. The dropping of the heaviness of earth plane illusion and the knowing of who you are cannot be conveyed by words. I just beg you to try it. The number of moments you build this power will determine the moment of your Freedom. You lift off and out and you are no longer encased. You know—it's done! You know you are God, always have been, could never be anything else, and in that wondrous moment, you know you have everything. The *only* thing I think worth doing is to build the power so you can *know*!

Part Two
INDIVIDUAL & GROUP EXERCISES

We often sit and spend hours listening to Bartholomew's
different messages. 'He' repeatedly tells us that *we* are
the way and the light, can be our *own* teachers, and
must walk our own path. 'He' gives us many tools
in the hope some of them will help us toward
our goal of Freedom. Just as we exercise our
physical bodies with different techniques,
so too, can we 'fine tune' our spiritual
bodies. The following section has
some of the 'spiritual exercises'
we have practiced in workshops over the years.

center

Some of the exercises involve visualization or require writing or the drawings of mandalas, so here is a brief word of explanation about the process and the materials required. It is obvious to keep a notebook and pen handy, but for the writing exercise it is also important to consider location and number of people involved. We hope that all the exercises will be used by groups, since we've found them so helpful in their original workshop situations. Visualizations can be done anywhere, and we urge you to be imaginative in choosing their locations. Any visualization can be greatly enhanced by a powerful setting.

And finally a word about mandala drawings. As we look at the variety of ways to meet and address the symbolic in our lives, we travel beyond the rational mind and find a shortcut to feeling and expression through the drawing of mandalas. We can draw on our own unique, individual combinations of color and abstract form to create the experience of ourselves as symbol-makers. Putting our feelings into color and the intuitive into form can produce 'feeling tones' with which we can visually dialogue with ourselves. The materials used for mandala drawings are crayons or oil and a large circle drawn on a good-sized piece of paper.

Now we have all the ingredients necessary to activate another level of consciousness. So then, let us begin.

THE
BALANCED
CROSS

For many centuries you have been living in your world with a powerful symbol. It is the symbol of the balanced cross. Long before the advent of Christianity, the symbol of this cross has been observed as one of the most strengthening symbols the world has to offer. Its explanation is very simple. You have at your constant disposal two streams of energy and the balanced cross is a reminder of this. One of them is a horizontal stream of energy. It is the one that connects you with all of the manifest world. It connects you with other people's egos, with the material plane, the emotional field, and with the mentalizations of life. The horizontal stream is what is constantly before your physical eyes. Since it is this stream that has fed you throughout centuries and lifetimes, the second, vertical stream of energy has been forgotten. Therefore, you have a very weakened balance point within you because it is through the forgotten vertical you connect with the Divine. So we will begin with an empowering exercise that will bring the vertical stream of energy into your awareness.

Tree Visualization

Stand and close your eyes, please. Visualize a wonderful array of branches and leaves reaching out of your torso and moving up into space as far as feels comfortable for you. These branches catch the light and power of the energy which is constantly moving in the Vastness. That light and power enters through the leaves and moves down into you. Your body is the trunk of this wondrous tree, and as the energy moves through you, it goes out the bottom of your feet, down deeply into the earth itself, as deeply into the earth as you feel is safe. These are your roots. What do these roots look like? Some of them might be thin, others thicker or more sturdy. Get a sense of them. Spend a few moments and get a real sense of what being this tree feels like. It is an important beginning.

Pause. Rest please.

Understand the basic law from which everything arises—
energy follows thought. Put another way, energy follows visualization, and put another way, power follows what you visualize. If
you create a visual and thoughtful link with the vertical stream of
energy, you will begin to manifest it daily your life. Many of you
are looking for a centering device. *The degree to which you want to
be centered is the degree to which you will be* . The reason you enjoy
the horizontal is the sense of motion you experience when your
ego energy moves out and blends with other similar energies, now
side to side, now backward and forward. It makes you feel alive, as
though you are 'doing' something. Let us experiment with how
that feels.

A Horizontal Movement

*Stand with your feet firmly planted on the ground. Bend
forward with your arms parallel to the ground. Now swing your
arms and torso right to left and back again.*

Pause.

*Notice that there is a sense of movement but not a strong
sense of centeredness. It is the feeling of movement you are
addicted to. But please, my friends, think about it. Do you want
this kind of motion endlessly, this motion of the ego that buffets
you from side to side? The world loves you. The world hates you.
You can have what you want, you can't have what you want. Back
and forth, side to side, this motion goes.*

Rest please, but keep standing.

The power of the vertical is so much stronger than the small,
horizontal motions you make. But you continue to think those
small back and forth motions are life. Eventually you must realize
even the more frantic of the horizontal motions are not enough.
What you are longing for are the vaster sweeps of energy that you
have all sensed moving through you on occasion. It is the incredible power of the vertical stream of energy that gives you a feeling
of groundedness. The horizontal can't contain too much of that
energy because you would simply fall right over. You have to
begin to empower yourself in a totally new way. So, let us now
attempt to experience the strength of the vertical. If you feel more

66

comfortable with your eyes closed, please close them.

The Vertical

Many of you have a spiritual quest that is very mental, which is fine, but it also needs to be brought down into the body. To do that, feel your feet planted firmly on the ground. Begin to move the rest of your body side to side. Keep gently moving and swaying until you feel a vertical plumb line that brings your body to center. Then just stop whenever you feel most aligned. Experience fully, in your body, how it feels to be centered and in alignment with the Above.

Please stand at ease.

As you experience that centered awareness, let us talk about a basic dilemma, the dilemma between wanting to have roots and the fear that you have none. You have been trained for centuries to ignore your roots. I am not talking about your cultural roots. I am talking about the roots that go down into the dark places of your being. The light, the beauty, and the wonder of the God-Self have been presented very well. What is fearful and has become increasingly fearful for mankind, is to acknowledge the roots and claim the ability to allow himself to feel the deep, dark parts of who he is. The most difficult thing for man today is to live at ease with a sense of the unknown. And that is exactly what you have to learn in order to be strong at all times and master of the moment. When you start incorporating, as part of the power of your life, the joy and the delight of learning how to welcome and dance with the unknown, you will become empowered. You will welcome the unknown as your brother or sister instead of pushing it away. You do this by simply beginning to affirm, "The unknown is my ally, my brother, my mystery. I welcome it!"

Roots are also those places that have to do with the chaotic part of your nature, the part of you that is unpredictable. They are a part you have been sitting on for many years because they are very unacceptable. They are not acceptable because they are not rational, and people grow very uncomfortable around the irrational. But you will never feel a total sense of your power until you you deeply feel and acknowledge those roots.

67

Roots

So with that awareness as a background, please envision again a very large and wondrous tree reaching up into the Vastness. Feel the power of the Vastness pouring down into you. Let the top of the tree get as high as you feel comfortable with. This is not an exercise that you figure out and then do the same way again and again. Some days your tree will go very, very high up into the Vastness and other days will barely get past the roof of your house. Go with your sensitivity and your intuitive responses because they will tell you what is appropriate for this moment. Envision your tree with the leaves catching all of the power and light of the Vastness and bringing it down through your head, into your body.

Pause.

When you get it into your body, take it very carefully through each one of the chakras along your spinal column and hold it there until you have felt some connection with each chakra. Feel the energy in your crown, forehead, throat, chest, solar plexus, abdomen, and sexual centers.

Pause.

Now, put your awareness into your feet. Feeling the energy in your feet, move it down into the roots that grow out of your feet, and on deep into the ground. Pay particular attention to the roots. Feel how deeply they go. Are some powerful? Are some frightening? What does the webwork of your root system look and feel like? Watch how it splays out and which tendrils are long and which ones are short. What are their shapes? When you are through, quietly take a seated position and maintain the awareness of the light and power of your tree as much as possible.

Pause until finished.

Drawing the Roots

It is now time to do the visual part of this exercise, which is the drawing. You see, my friends, much of your energy is compacted down deep in your roots so that energy is not available in your life. The roots are too far away and inaccessible to you. It's as

68

if there are blockages and you can't get things to flow. When you decide you are willing and ready to face the unacceptable desires, thoughts, and actions you find there, you begin to loosen up the field around them and the blockages are washed away. The unexamined self is always in jeopardy because those unexamined parts of you can come up at unexpected moments. But when you understand and face those secret places in your being, and examine them in the way you examine other parts of your life, there are no surprises. Life is no longer a scary proposition. You know when you are in one of those frightening areas and you can 'hold your ground' and feel strong. This drawing is one way to examine your hidden roots.

Use a large piece of paper and at least seven colors in your drawing. Begin at the top of your paper and draw those roots you have just seen and felt. Please, not just one root. Fall deeply into them. They won't all necessarily take the shape you think roots look like. What you are trying to do is to reach down inside yourself and feel the mysterious part of you that would come out spontaneously if you really felt it was safe and acceptable to allow it. What are those things deep down in there? What would those hidden roots be like? What kind of a person would you be if you really and truly knew that everything you chose to do and say was acceptable? Not just tolerated, but accepted and delighted in, and entered into. Be daring, be courageous. Some of these roots may be painful or frightening. But they are your children—your creations, and as such, can be totally understood and accepted. Be aware that when you bring them to your consciousness through the symbolic motion of this drawing, you release their energy.

I repeat, these tendrils do not necessarily have to look like roots. They can take any number of shapes. Go deeply inside yourself and discover what they feel like. Then sense their color and shape and put it all down somewhere in this drawing.

SUGGESTION: *We find that music helps in this part of the exercise. Choose it with an awareness of what you are reaching for. Something powerful in the beginning and sweet towards the end would be appropriate. This exercise takes at least thirty minutes. If some people*

Infinity Visualization

Now for the last round of visualization. Please rise and practice feeling the energy of the Vastness entering from above you. Pull it through your physical body and down into the ground. Feel the continuation of your energy field moving deeply down into the earth.

Short pause.

Visualize the energy going deeper still, cupping itself around and encircling that wonderful ball of fire in the center of the earth. See it moving back up, passing through your root system and entering your body. Feel it sweep through the branches and leaves and out into the vault of the heavens. Those wonderful pictures you make of the figure 8's are exactly what I am talking about. And there in the center is where the two arms of the cross meet, and that center is in your body. You are a conductor of this power.

Short pause.

When you are through, please be seated and maintain the awareness of this vertical stream of energy as much as possible.

Pause until completed.

If you feel like you want to experience more power, begin to do this exercise on a regular basis. You can do it as you wash the dishes, wait in line, or walk down the street. You can do it anywhere. As you integrate this simple technique into your life as a physical reality, you will begin to feel the power because energy *does* follow thought.

If you wish your life to be more powerful, creative, extending, and delightful, spend some time acknowledging your willingness to change, and begin experiencing the vertical energy that is always there. The horizontal ego is very compelling, but you have all learned that ego energy, although satisfying at times, often produces its polar opposite, which is dissatisfaction. There is no need to do away with the horizontal. What you are looking for is a

70

balance between both so you can empower yourself. And to do that, you need to experience the inner dependability, unconditional wonder and power of the vertical stream of energy.

IN
THE
MOMENT

Here's a simple little exercise that can quickly show how many of us spend our time 'in the moment.' If you can manage, give yourself a day with it. If not, a few hours should suffice. —Ed.

The assignment is this: You may talk all you want, but you may not speak about anything that has to do with the past or the future. You may say what you wish, but it must relate only to **the present moment**. In doing this, you will easily see where you spend your time. Interesting, is it not?

A
STREAM OF
UNCONSCIOUS
CONSCIOUSNESS

The following is a short exercise that takes a long time, a lot of perseverance, and a stiff shot of courage. It is not easy to sit with yourself for six hours and watch what the mind creates. But if you can, you will never feel the same about your mind again. The mind is the most complex part of the psyche and has many brilliant facets. Each facet also casts a shadow, so please be kind to your-selves, appreciate the sparkle, and have compassion for the darkness. A little humor will go a long way in appreciating this exercise. —Ed.

The exercise requires six hours of nonstop writing, which in the end can enable you to see the garbage and the beauty in your mental consciousness. When you fill page upon page with *every thought* that comes into your mind, you will become aware of why your life is the way it is. Your thoughts are what you visualize constantly and they are what you manifest in your world. After six hours of uninterrupted writing, you will find your mental defenses are weakened, and from the clarity gained by watching this process, you will truly see how *you manifest your own world.* Most of you long to believe in manifestation, but at the same time are terrified to because you are afraid your negative thoughts might harm others. This will not happen because your thoughts create *your* world. Those of you who talk about transformation and really want it will benefit by putting yourselves under this writing discipline for six steady hours. From this exercise, you will realize you have created your life the way it is now, therefore you also have the ability to create it a different way.

The following is a description and some suggestions for setting up the writing exercise. It is only the starting point for a number of different possibilities.

Having a group do this exercise together is helpful. Not only is the group energy supportive when you get tired, but the proximity of other people will stimulate your mind in ways that being alone cannot. Having others present will also engage your ego and help you stay with the exercise.

knowledge   **75**

A quiet, comfortable place with room to move around in is an advantage. Try to pick a time of day when the people are not too tired. We did the exercise for six hours. Five hours or seven hours would work just as well. The object is to keep writing long enough to tire the mind. It helped not to eat a heavy meal before the exercise and to have liquids to drink during it. Around the fourth and fifth hour, a slump set in. Stretching and movement were encouraged. Sleeping was not. We realized that sleep would be a great way of escaping.

*When Bartholomew said continuous writing of **everything** that came into the mind, 'he' meant it. And therein lies the difficulty. Here's a short sample of the exercise:*

Why did I commit to this I don't know what to write my nose itches I wish that fat guy would sit still oh no I forgot my father's birthday again boy am I thirsty I'll never last six hours I wonder what time it is I wonder why I always seem to forget his birthday . . .

*And finally, when you're done, take all the sheets of paper, the few uncovered gems as well as the reams of triviality, and with great love and due ceremony, destroy them. Some of us wanted to hang onto the gems. We felt that after all our hard work, we had earned them. Bartholomew said that all thoughts are the same (which we didn't like hearing!) and that the idea was to begin a practice of dropping down **past** the surface-mind that had produced these pages into our deep, inner space, and to begin to think, sense, and feel the nudges of another energy field that rested within us. This was 'his' final statement. —Ed.*

Dear friends, let us assume for the moment that you have two minds—ego/limited/frightened mind, and Vast/Unlimited/Compassionate Mind. The first mind reflects the world that your ego has created, and contains only unreal thoughts. They arise from the limited, and die into the limited. They cannot hurt you because they are not real. The second Mind arises from God, from the Source, from the Changeless. These 'thoughts' move outward spontaneously from the center of you *when you turn within and ask that they come forward*! They are the thoughts of the Heart of God, and are in your heart also. All is well, my beloved ones, because

God thoughts are the only Reality that endures. Other thoughts will not endure because they are not eternal—they are as passing clouds in an endless sky. Do not be afraid.

PATTERNS
FROM
THE PAST

The area of consciousness within the physical body that causes most of you the greatest pain is the area of the heart. Not the heart of Love, of Divine compassion, but that part of the heart which reflects the anguish you believe to be true of the separated self. You believe yourselves to be separated and, therefore, need from others what you perceive to be outside of yourself. In that process, instead of being appreciative of what you *do* have, you spend a lot of time wanting the things you aren't getting. So, we are going to allow the deprived, yearning part in all of you to state very clearly what it is your heart didn't get, who it didn't get it from, and what you want to say to the person who didn't give it to you. Please realize you didn't get your deepest needs met outside yourself and you aren't going to! If you could wake up to that reality, you would quit going down the same road looking for the same piece of cheese which has long since deteriorated and passed away. It is an endless, repetitive pattern that I ask you, as a mature consciousness, to acknowledge and then put aside. The game of life was not set up to be won by getting your needs met by others. Every one of you has been hurt and, at the same time, has hurt others.

So, in order to hear the Divine heartbeat that constantly sounds in your awareness, let us cast away all the dreams of what you thought you wanted or needed, because they are not what will make your life dynamic, alive, exciting, and peace-filled. What you need is a constant connection with your Deep Self. You must clear away the clutter of other images, other wishes, and all unfulfilled desires.

Mandala on Past Patterning

Materials:
Photographs of people that you have difficulty with and/or those you love and would like to love more deeply
Paper with large circle
Crayons or oil pastels

Place the pictures of those persons who you know you have unfinished business with to the left side of your circle. On the right, place the pictures of those who you love and care for and wish to deepen your love for. Some people will fall into both categories, so place them in the middle.

This exercise may prove difficult for some of you. It is an emotional experience of the deepest kind to finally decide to let go of a bond that is *negative*, because some of you are afraid that the negative is the *only* way you are connected. And to let that negative bond dissolve might mean there is nothing between you at all. This is not the truth. You can never bond with anyone *only* through the negative. The thing bonding anyone is the heart. *The heart does the connecting and the mind does the separating.* Even if you have difficulty with someone, you are bonded to them somewhere in your heart in the truest and clearest sense possible. The pain is caused by falling onto the grid of your ego and being burned by the power of that grid. In order to drop *through* and into the depths of compassion, we have to work our way through the openings of the 'ego grid.'

*Pick up the deepest blue and purple colors you have. Without thought, color in the **bottom** of your circle. Now select four people from either side of your circle. Please note: If you don't have four people, you can work with the number you do have. Put those pictures in front of you, or, if you don't have pictures, place each individual in the front of your consciousness.*

Look at the remaining space in your circle. The people you have selected will occupy varying amounts of that space depending on their importance in your life. Choose the first person, and do not look only at how difficult it is with that person, but how much space, from the time of your first experience with them until this moment, the person has taken up in your life. You know which one has been the biggest problem and the greatest delight, so give them the largest shape. You do this by selecting the color or combination of colors you intuitively feel they represent. Use them to make a shape that reflects the person's impact on your life. Your unconscious can do this easily, so get your conscious mind out of the way. You can do so by feeling, not thinking.

80

Now take the rest of the people you have chosen, determine how much space they occupy, and place their color and shape in your drawing. Again, be sure this is done from a deep, intuitive level, not from your mind.

Pause until finished.

Now draw a crisscross grid over the shapes of the people in your mandala.

Short pause.

In your consciousness, allow your old pains around those people to slip through the ego grid you have created into the blue-purple at the bottom of your paper. What you do by this action is inform your conscious mind you are ready and willing to drop away from the old and create a new, gentle and loving relationship with these important people. That blue-purple color represents the Vastness of your Being, and it is large enough to dissipate those old griefs. So, with consciousness, this is a good time to release them.

Pause until completed.

THE
NATURAL
WORLD

*This series of exercises was taken from material pre-
sented at the nature workshop in Taos in the summer
of 1986. We were gathered on the rim of a canyon overlooking the
Rio Pueblo, perched amidst sage and cactus under the vastness of a
high desert sky. Bartholomew began by reintroducing us to the natural
world.* —Ed.

Man has been systematically trained, by his intellect, to
separate from the forces that are participating with him in this
grand earth plane experiment. The natural world has the same
deep objective as you do, which is to take the wondrous gossamer
power you call the Divine and bring it into form on the earth
plane. The human vehicle has its own kind of expression, as does
the rest of creation. There is no hierarchy whatsoever. It is simply
a question of what your particular assignment is, given the kind of
equipment you happen to have. In man's struggle to identify himself, he has, for the most part, placed himself above the natural
order of things. And this is a very limiting and lonely position.

There are energy vortexes awash on the earth plane that
delight in caressing you with their power in order to make your
job here easier. It was out of an integrated Oneness this whole
wonderful explosion of earth plane consciousness came into
being. It wasn't some terrible mistake which resulted in your being
stuck here with no way to get out. Please realize you have cut
yourself off from many natural nourishing qualities that could
support you during difficult times.

What you are looking for is to be nourished constantly and
to nourish those you love constantly. To say there is something
wrong with you because you wish to be nourished puts you out of
harmony with the entire universe. This planet, those rocks, this
sage, everything calls out to the rest of the natural world to be
nourished. To nourish is to join, to integrate, to be whole. And
nourishment flows in many directions.

four directions   **83**

When you take responsibility for allowing the vast powers of the natural to nourish you, you will become a lot less demanding in wanting other people and things in your manifest universe to provide you with nourishment. So if you are ready to experience a sense of total well-being, rightness, and absolute delight in your life as it is manifesting now, this lesson is for you. Each of you stands as an explosive point of power, and coming into you from different directions, at all times, are amazing other energies. They are ever-present and they are ever in motion. Those energies are not very useful until you start identifying the play of each energy field upon you. For now, we will call those energy fields the Four Directions.

Each direction has something to say to you, something it wants from you, and something it wants to give to you. The voices are intimate, soft and gentle, filled with the desire to have you listen, and in turn, listen to you. This communication goes both ways. These energies need to hear from you, just as you need to hear from them. We are talking about a *reciprocal* orchestration of power. So then, let us see if we can expand our consciousness to become aware of the particular energy associated with each direction.

THE EAST

The first direction is the direction of the east. The east corresponds to the element of air, to dawn, the mind, spring, the pale airy colors of white and violet, to the eagle and other high-flying birds, and to the power to know. *The material symbol of the east is the sword. It is the double-sided sword of decision. With awareness, the mind can use this tool to cut through illusion to the truth.*

So, please close your eyes and become centered in whatever way is meaningful to you. Breathe deeply and be conscious of the air as it flows in and out of your lungs. Feel that air as the breath of the Divine. Breathe it in as a life force, as inspiration, as creation. When you exhale, let your own breath merge with the wind and clouds, with the great currents of air that sweep over land and sea as the earth revolves on its axis.

Pause.

There are few symbols in the human consciousness which

resound with as much meaning as do those of the winged ones. The bird can be said to be the vehicle that takes your prayers and carries them to heaven. And if the bird is black, it is also able to fly *between* the worlds. A black bird has the ability to fly from the light to the dark, from the known to the unknown, from the manifest to the unmanifest. I think it a rare human being who has not dreamt of birds in one way or another, and an unfeeling human who has watched the flight of a bird and not yearned to be able to do what the bird does with such simple grace, which is to leave the earth plane and fly.

So let us now talk about the gift the bird symbolizes in your consciousness. If what you want more than anything else is to fly free from the limitations you feel on the earth plane, soar through space and break into another realm of consciousness, then the winged ones can be used to aid you. You know that energy follows thought, and most of your thoughts, most of the time, are quite earthbound. This is not because there is something wrong with you, but because everything in your environment keeps telling you that you are limited, stuck and unable to move. And when you look at a bird, your heart yearns to fly.

Meditation on Expansion

Please take a comfortable position lying down. With your body in full contact with the earth, we will be able to use it to push off into the Vastness. You can begin to develop the ability to 'lift off and out' of whatever seems to entrap you, and break free of that particular gravitational field of belief or limitation.

Concentrate on your breath. Become aware of your breath as it moves throughout your body. Feel it filling your cells, all your cells, your whole body. Then extend that awareness to the energy around your physical body. Feel the ground, hear the sounds, acknowledge the strength of the energies surrounding you. Take your time. Feel the energy around you and under you. Now feel your energy push off from the earth and move upward and out-ward. Feel the lift-off! Feel your energy moving skyward. Your spirit has the ability to fly free. Do this until you have the feeling of moving out. Energy follows thought. When you feel yourself to be stuck, hurt, angry, confused, or fearful, if you will stop a moment, feel what is happening around you, 'push off' from the earth and feel yourself moving upward, you will begin to separate from that particular emotion, fear, or feeling. You will not reconcile your entire life process, but you can for that moment, fly free of any particular limitation and remember, **Freedom is one moment's liberation after another**.

Pause until you feel a completion.

When you do this exercise, you will find that whatever particular dilemma has been engaging your consciousness will not have the same grip on you that it had the moment before. Every time you are locked into a pattern of restriction, you can leap against it and start flying. The more times you do it, the more you will get the feeling of a spiritual 'lift-off.' If you don't want to be trapped, then just move out. You don't have to change anyone. You don't have to change anything. You can use the winged ones as a symbol of conscious freedom from your limitations and as a reminder of your journey Home.

Wave Meditation

The next symbol I ask you to dwell upon is spoken of as a wave of energy. That wave is now moving across this planet. With your awareness in the east, envision coming out of that direction, as immense, as buoyant, as filled with Light as you can possibly make it, a wonderful undulating wave thundering across the mesa, coming upon us, and moving on. Would you please spend a few moments doing this and make sure, as you visualize it, the wave moves through you. Feel this wave and join with it. Make it real.

Pause.

The wave has something to say, and you have something to hear. Allow it. Feel it. Now, let us go one step further. With this overwhelming wave of energy coming into your life, I ask you to dwell on two questions: **What would you like the wave to take out of your life, and what would you like it to bring into it?** Be as specific as you can. Take pencil and paper and list those things you would have this wave take away that you do not want. Write every emotional, mental, physical, and spiritual limitation you are

86

ready to release. Take hold of all those parts of your psyche that you are ready to have go on their way and put them on your paper. Then, with the same honest scrutiny, also write down those things you would like to see appear in your life. When you are finished with your list, please set your paper aside and we will go on to the next direction.

THE SOUTH

We now move to the second direction, the direction of the south. The south corresponds to the element of fire, to summer, the sun, to energy, fiery reds and oranges, to the lion, and the quality of will. The material symbol of this direction is the staff. It is used to invoke the Divine, to channel energy, and to direct power.

Once again, please close your eyes and become aware of your breath. Let your breath pass in and out of your body. Become conscious of the individual cells and the spark within each nerve as they fire from synapse to synapse. Be aware of the slow combustion within each cell as food burns to release energy. Dwell on your own inner fire and blend with the remembrance of the gentle fire of a candle, with the warmth of an open fire, the cold fire of lightning and star-light, a fiery sun, and become one with the blazing Spirit of the Divine.

Pause.

Let us first focus on the material symbol of this direction, which is the staff. Throughout history, when you go on a journey, you have taken along something to hold you up, something to lean upon, something that you feel will help you on your way. And this object is the staff. Please remember the staff has been, and can still be, used as a staff of power to connect heaven and earth. As you walk with it, the staff channels the power of the heavens through your hand and grounds it in the earth. If you choose to create one for yourself, here are some suggestions.

The Rod of Power

Start with a piece of wood that is tapered and at least a foot taller than you are. You get your staff from a living tree, so please select it carefully and cut it with gratitude. Replacing the limb with a gift for the tree or bush would be appropriate. Leave some corn meal, tobacco, or a crystal along with a prayer of thanks. Grasp the wood in your strongest hand and find the place where it feels most comfortable. This will become the place of balance on your staff. Holding it at this point, swing the staff around until you can feel which end is heaviest. Then, an inch at a time, trim the wood from either or both ends until you feel the staff to be a natural, balanced extension of you.

This is a tool you can also play with, and if you will begin to consider it thusly, you can discover the absolute joy in planning a day that includes your staff. It can be walking in a meadow, through some valley, or even in a nearby park. As you do this, you will begin to understand you are a transmission pole, that *you yourself* connect earth with heaven and the staff is a material reminder of that connection.

Meditation on the Will

So now that we have this tool, let us see if we can dispel some of the doubt present in several of you concerning the validity of this exercise. Take up the steaff, grasp it with one hand, and become still and aware of your breath. Take all the time you need. Slowly, slowly, breathe in and out.
Short pause.

My friends, as you do this, give yourself an opportunity to feel something unseen, mysterious, miraculous. Many of you do not believe in God as a moving Force you can turn to and have manifest. So let's see if you can use this exercise to feel that Force. Just keep your awareness on your hand, on the staff and yourself, and see what happens.

Follow the breath in your body. With each in-breath, let the energy and your awareness move down the arm holding the staff. Breathe your consciousness into your hand and become aware of feeling the staff as a 'power pole.' Become one with the staff and feel the power of the energy moving through it. Be aware of your-self as a similar channel of energy. You can change ideas into reality, concept into form, and spirit into matter. Feel your own power of creation, your own ability to be an agent of change. Touch on

88

*your will, your power to set a goal, whether inner or outer, and
work towards it. Dwell on what that goal would be, and become
aware of the firmness of your intention. Don't forget—breathe in,
breathe out. Follow the power. Feel the power. Feel your power
moving in you.*

Pause until finished.

The Inner Fire of Transformation

Now let us focus on the element of this direction, which is
fire. In your modern age, you have created a mechanism called an
atomic reactor. This is interesting because it is similar to a process
that happens in your bodies. Your physical bodies contain a series
of ever present, ongoing chain reactions. But that is not how you
experience yourselves. You experience yourselves much the same
from day to day. If you could see yourselves psychically, you
would observe you are always in a state of explosion, of change, as
one synapse fires to the next and the next. This is important
because it is the basis upon which transformation takes place.
Transformation comes about when you quiet yourself down so
you can begin to *feel* the chain reaction going on in your body.

The point here is simple. By dwelling on the idea that within
your body, within every cell, is an explosive point of power which
is always firing, you can remember **nothing has to stay the same.**
When your life is dismal, it is because you think you are never
going to be able to change it, life is never going to get any better.
Then comes the feeling of helplessness and depression. Depression is present when you feel no hope of a way out, when you look
around your universe and see no door to open. So you go to your
mind and try to talk yourself out of your depression, but
discouragement is often what you find.

There is a more immediate way to get out of depression and
help can come from the direction of the south. This is how it
works.

*Wherever you are, take a moment to become still. Lying
down or standing up, become aware of your breath. Then dwell
on the idea that your body contains the transformative energy to
make the changes you need. Starting with your feet and moving*

89

upward throughout your body, become aware of the wondrous minute explosions of your synapse responses taking place. Follow them up and all the way out the top of your head. Do this over and over. At first it will be 'imagination,' but you will, with practice, begin to feel the reaction, the new life taking shape.

When you work with this idea, something very simple happens. You take your mind off of depression, which is helpful because then you have the space to detach from it. But even more important, *it sparks off another re-action.* It puts some other energy into motion.

When your mind is depressed, you often think your body has to be depressed also. You give it pills to knock it out. You lay it down and try to forget about it. But since the body is *not* what is depressed, you can begin to relieve the problem when you start your body moving into a new enlivened state. When your body is delighting in itself, there comes a point at which you pull yourself out of the depression. My friends, with all sincerity, if you find that you are in a mental state of difficulty, do not compound it by *throwing your body in with it.* Pull your body out of the dilemma, claim its vigor, its life, its wonder, and start working with what you have. Like other things, depression comes and goes. Please don't be so depressed over being depressed! You can actively use the symbol of the south in a simple, direct way to become aware of the fire in your own bodies. This in turn will help you burn through the problems of your mind.

Fire Ritual

At this point, a fire had been started in a circle of rocks nearby. If you or your group wish to actively duplicate this ritual, you can create a similar circular fire with rocks, a round pan or bowl, or any other container or material that utilizes a circle. The circle is the symbol of wholeness, completion, and totality, and is a powerfully helpful form for rituals of this sort. —Ed.

We are now going to perform a ritual that involves the element from the direction of the south. This, of course, is fire, and we are going to use the transformative power of fire to release those things on your list from the east you would like to take out of your life, and bring in those things you would like to see in it.

Before we begin, I would like to give you some suggestions on how to prepare yourself for any ritual. *In the intention is the result.* With the maximum intention comes your victory. You do not know how to remove all the impediments from your life and you do not need to. Your responsibility is to set the intention to do so. With intention, you tell the universe what it is you want from it. And since the universe loves you, it will give you what you *truly* want, so please make sure your intention is for the highest you know in that moment.

*Stand near the fire, feeling yourself centered. Gather your power and the energy that surrounds you and pull it into you. Consciously pull it into you and feel the expansion and power in your body. Then, with all of the intensity you possess, state your present intention to release all of the strands you have listed as wanting removed from your life. (This can be done silently or out loud.) Now, consciously and openly ask for the new to replace them. Put your list on the fire and let your awareness become part of that burning. With fire and smoke come the release **of the energy of those desires.** And when the burning is complete, be grateful. Send your gratitude up and out with the ashes.*

Your intention to release your creations is all that is necessary. You can join with a power greater than yourself to unbind those patterns you no longer want. You don't have to do it by yourselves. Intention is the single, strongest tool that a warrior possesses. Make your intention clear and firm, and I promise you, the help will be there.

THE WEST

The third direction is the west. From the west we learn about our emotional bodies. This direction corresponds to the element of water, the season of autumn, to twilight, cool blues, soft grays and deep purples, to the sea, fish and dolphins, to the power to risk. The west gives us the courage to face our deepest emotions. The material symbol of the west is the cup or chalice.

We left our perch on the rim of the canyon at midday and made our way down a rock fall to the river below. The recording equipment was left behind, so Mary-Margaret was asked to recall this direction both from her own experience and as the channel of Bartholomew. —Ed.

Today we walked down to the river and spent the afternoon listening and learning from its wisdom. We waded across the swift-moving water and found ourselves comfortably seated in a field of clover. Here Bartholomew spoke about the third direction, the direction of the west, the element of water.

Letting Go

'He' began by having us sit alongside the riverbank and alternate between looking at the water, and closing our eyes to feel and hear the water as it moved. 'He' said the direction of the west could teach us to 'let go,' and in the movement of the river we could see how to let go of the *encumbrances* we have in and around us. We practiced this, alternating between using our eyes as a sensory organ to feel and caress the water in motion, then closing them and allowing our ears and awareness to sense the water flowing strongly in front of us. Many of us, as we talked about it later, began to get the sense of *energy in motion*.

It proved to be a very successful exercise because it gave us a way to really touch on and blend with something powerful that was letting go all the time. The Rio Pueblo is a very beautiful, but small, fast moving river and we could feel it letting go, moment by moment, letting go and moving on. It was, for me, a very exhilarating exercise, perhaps the first really exhilarating time I have had sitting by rivers. Bartholomew kept insisting this was not to be a *mental idea*, that we should not be thinking things like, "The water is moving, going around the rock and letting go here and there." 'He' told us it had to be a physical joining with the water and its movement. Through the sound, the movement and the power, we blended with the water, and the feeling of its motion was a delightful experience.

The focus of the 'letting go' was of the emotional, the west. For example, I found it helpful to practice letting go of small irritations, like being aware of the little bug caught in my hair and then letting that irritation go, and so on. It proved to be a very effective device. It was exciting, much different than watching the

92

ocean, for example, which is a whole other experience. The teaching of a fast river or stream is in the swift movement of nonclinging water, which is absolutely delightful. There was no judgment, so I found it very helpful, and the whole afternoon was really a beautiful experience.

THE NORTH

The final direction is the north, which corresponds to the body and the element of earth. It is the direction of Spirit, midnight, mystery, the unseen, the season of winter, black, brown, and the deep green of growing things. From the north comes the power to listen as well as speak, the power of silence. *The symbol of the north is the circle.*

It is through a circle you were born onto this earth plane and it is through a circle you are born into other worlds as well. The north is the point of entry into the black light, the place where you can be born again in the *whole* sense. Most of you have a tendency to believe you are going to be reborn into brilliant light, so when I say 'black light' or 'darkness' a certain fear comes in. Instead of being afraid, please entertain the idea you are on your way to something much deeper than you can imagine, and let yourself move in that direction.

One of the most difficult beliefs you have to overcome is the belief that somehow you are not ready to be born into a state of higher awareness. On the earth plane, things have a gestation or germination period, so there is planted within you the unconscious idea that it requires a certain amount of time before you can be 'born'. You usually believe you are not ready for this state, but you also haven't really defined what is needed to be ready. As long as you believe an undetermined length of time is necessary to be born anew, you will not step into the circle. Begin to claim the desire that you *are ready* to be whole, to enter a new state of awareness, *NOW*, and you will begin the process of having this come about.

Every one of you has, at this time, in this moment, the ability to break through into some kind of new understanding about yourself. I am not talking about total Enlightenment. There are those of you who do not yet want to be totally One with God because you have not finished playing in your separated way. So, to whatever extent you wish wholeness for yourself now, let us move that much closer to the goal.

It is great fun to know the part of you which can stand in the midst of chaos and feel a point of centered power. One of the ways to empower your life is to acknowledge *you* are that point from which your power moves, and *you* have the ability to center the power within your body. How wonderful it is to know that you, the warrior, can center this power at your command! So, right now, be the warrior and grasp the chance to break through to a new awareness, even if only for a moment.

Black Hole Meditation and Mandala

To help you do this, first face the north and become still and grounded in whatever way is most comfortable for you. Feel the weight of your body in contact with the earth. Be aware of your bones and the pull of gravity. Merge your consciousness with the weight of the earth and growing things. Slowly merge with and become rooted in the earth.

Pause.

From this deep, grounded position, stretch your awareness up and out. As you move out, there is a small speck off in the distance that attracts your attention. See it clearly, in front of you. Allow your awareness to move toward it. Feel your awareness thrusting forward, gathering speed. As you approach, notice the speck has actually become a Black Hole. It is a 'doorway' opening into another level of reality. Take a moment to ask yourself what you would want to see there. What are you working toward, yearning for? **Claim what it is you truly want in your life that is new, different, and exciting.**

Short pause.

Now move to the Black Hole and 'poke' your awareness through the opening. Really poke through the circle. Look around. What do you see, feel or sense? Take your time to let the impressions fill you. Be as definite in your sensing as you can. Is it

94

light? A figure? A feeling? A release? Expansion? Peace? Power?
What?

Pause.

*Now we are going to record these impressions in a mandala. Some of you formulate things better with words. So begin first with a word. For example, if one of the things you immediately felt was expansion, use the word. Jot them all down in the margin of your paper and then put them into the kind of form that best expresses the feelings. Others of you work best when you place your impressions directly on paper, so after you look around, start picking up colors that appeal to you and put them down in whatever form comes to you. Do not be tricked into thinking this is an art exercise. It is a concrete way to **see your inner expressions**. You have the ability to express your feelings through color and form, so use this method to record your experience of another level of reality.*

Pause until completed.

This exercise helps you to define where you want to journey, and, out of that knowledge, your deep Self begins to participate in the process. You cannot do this alone, and this is one of many methods to put the call out. When clarity is there, the Divine can move to help. And together you will come Home.

LEVEL
33

This exercise will allow us to move into the realm of imagination. When we do, an immediate mental question will arise: "If what we are about to do can't be rationally proven, how can I believe it is valid?" I would like you to entertain the idea that there must be *some* reason to choose what you visualize out of the millions of alternatives. If imagination were simply random ideas, then none of the symbols that you choose as a group should repeat themselves. Yet all over the world, through the centuries, we find the same symbols appearing again and again. They appear in ancient legends as well as modern dreams. You are not really on your own to create just anything out of imagination. The thing that you will select to imagine is that which best guides you to your desired end.

So remember, you are not working out of an ignorant space within your psyche. You have available to you an amazing well of understanding and knowledge, and you simply go and take a cup of what you need. All day, all night, through all your years, you go to those wells of understanding within your being and make use of them. Please understand, imagination is an incredibly important and vital method of aligning yourself with your own truth, and it becomes *intimately* yours.

Let us begin.

Level '33' Exercise

All numbers have deep meanings you are rarely aware of, and every number speaks in its own individual way. So I want you to **think** *of the number 33. It is not just a number. Thirty-three is a power which represents a state of consciousness. Let us not call it anything else. Right now it is simply Level 33. I would like you to take a moment and get the feeling of power around the number 33. As you think of this power, imagine yourself at the bottom of a ladder. Imagine starting to climb up the ladder toward Level 33. Feel the numbers as you pass them and feel the exhilaration of the climb. Just do this quietly, and when you have reached Level 33,*

perfection; harmony   **97** *simply raise your hand briefly.*

Pause until everyone has acknowledged finishing.

*Level 33 is a flat platform and all around you is openness.
Please visualize this carefully. Look down at your feet and see your
feet, which are bare, placed firmly on a piece of transparent material that looks like glass. Look around as you stand there, and see
the openness and feel the softness and power of your surroundings. Now look overhead. See the blueness that appears to be sky.
Look closer. In truth you are inside a wondrous sphere, and you
stand on a platform in its center looking up at the top of a sky-
blue dome. The feeling is of amazing security. It is familiar and it
is safe. Now look again at your feet and visualize them clearly in
your mind. Begin to walk with sure steps, watching your feet, to
the edge of this transparent platform. Now, JUMP!*

Pause.

*Without analyzing, pick up your paper and write what you
experienced. What did you **feel**?*

NOTE: *It is helpful, after the writing is completed, to take a
short break and have people share what they saw and felt in this exercise.
It has been our observation, in a group situation, that several people will
have similar experiences.* —Ed.

If the only thing you saw after you jumped were objects,
then you weren't on Level 33. But don't worry, all levels are safe
and you can always go back and try again. Out of all the things
you could have experienced, many of you in the end came to similar things. Why? Could it be there is such a thing as Level 33?
Could it be you were able collectively to go to Level 33 and begin
to experience another reality as you went up the ladder and
jumped off the platform? Please do not think you are making
these things up. You are only experiencing what is real. Level 33 is
a valid reality and I took you there because it has no shape and
form that you can grasp. There is nothing to hang on to. So when
you jump from the platform, instead of depending on your visual
sense for understanding, you find you must go to your feelings.
Level 33 has nothing to do with shape and form, it has to do with
sensing and feeling.

This exercise can be an important alternative for people who have difficulty meditating. When some people sit in meditation, instead of quieting the mind, they are continually concerned with the same kinds of thoughts. One way to bypass that difficulty is to go up to Level 33 and jump off. You will find, instead of being locked into the same thought patterns, you will begin to sense your feelings, and the feelings will quiet your mind. Another way in which Level 33 can be helpful is in solving problems. You can take yourself and some problem to Level 33 and jump off with it. The feelings you get around the problem as you descend bring about clarity and resolution.

Now, let's not just talk about this. Let's do it. Let's see if you can take a problem and go to Level 33 and have it make a difference. Start with a simple problem, for this technique, like any other, takes practice.

Start with something personal. For instance, if you've ever felt anger, jealousy, or worthlessness towards yourself or others, get into the feeling very intensely and ask the question, "How do I end this?" That is what you really want to know, isn't it? So the problem or dilemma arises out of an action or emotion, in this case. Spend a few moments now feeling out the situation you wish to take to Level 33. **You will not have the same experience that you had the last time.**

Short pause.

Problem Solving on Level '33'

Now visualize your problem as clearly as you can and take it into yourself as you stand at the foot of your ladder. Make your ascent and spend a little time on your platform looking out at the openness of the dome. It is very important to visualize the platform carefully and, most of all, to see your feet clearly. That is the touchstone that makes this experience a reality instead of imagination. See your feet and feel them planted solidly as you walk. Even though you know what you are going to do, walk with power, awareness, and the open invitation to receive a direction in which to move with your dilemma. As you fall or drift or fly off the edge of your platform, pay attention to feeling, not to thought. As you float with your problem, you also float with the solution. Out of the feeling will come either a word or a short phrase that will point the way out of your dilemma. Just drift with this word or phrase and go as far as you can with it.

Pause until finished.

For those of you who experienced a helpful shift in your awareness, remember the usefulness of this tool. The psyche is very literal and speaks in firm terms. It is not going to be abstract and spiritually symbolic. It is going to be direct because it is *you* who wants the answer and your psyche is your close friend.

Part Three
SYMBOLS, ALLIES & MYTHS

A very alive and empowered tool for awakening to our Deep
Selves is discovered through activating the dormant symbols
within us. Bartholomew is of tremendous assistance in
guiding us in the practice of making visible the invisi-
ble ideas and qualities that we have hidden in our
psyches. 'He' tells us we have our own different,
individual symbols that reflect the 'unseen'
energies within us, such as joy, pain, love,
or anger. 'He' clarifies time and again
how to find and read these symbols,
whether we choose to draw mandalas, engage in visual meditations, pull to us our ally,
or explore dreams.

heaven

SYMBOLS

Symbols are also available to us in the world we see. The natural symbols of the circle of the sun and the triangle of the mountain are both spoken of eloquently in the ancient Chinese Book of Changes, the I Ching. We can look further to nature as a dependable teacher. The animal kingdom has much to share with us through such things as the symbolic flight of the eagle, the earthbound snake, and the playfulness of the dolphin. Hence, we can look to the winged ones, the four leggeds, the water dwellers, and the mythological for insight and guidance. Clearly the material available daily to us is nearly unending. So welcome to the world of symbols, a world that surrounds you and waits patiently to teach you.

*T*he following material and exercises are drawn largely from the transcripts of workshops held over the past four years. The information has been extensively edited and rearranged to form a more condensed version of what Bartholomew has to share. I was surprised and delighted to witness there was no contradiction in the material over the years, nor were there any large gaps in information. This section of the book does not contain the total information presented in a workshop, by any means. Each workshop is an entity unto itself.

They take place in a weekend setting, at which time Bartholomew, as an energy orchestrator, opens us up to newer, vaster, inner possibilities we have not been acknowledging on our own. 'He' has often said 'he' would love to work with us while we sit in silence for two days, but we find this too difficult an assignment. Therefore, 'he' engages us through techniques and activities while 'he' works silently with each individual's energy field. To me, the weekend workshops are a charged reminder of what I truly want: deep, constant love in my life, and I'll gladly accept all the reminders and help I can get.

NOTE: As part of this section, Bartholomew had included instructions for a mandala drawing. It would be helpful to have a piece of paper with a large circle drawn on it and a box of crayons or oil pastels ready before you begin. A notebook and pen will also be needed. —Ed.

In order to activate a symbol so it can be useful, it is necessary to place that symbol outside of you so you can respond to it. This kind of activity has been known by you since the days when you made circles of stone and placed yourself in the middle of them, when you made towers and put bells in them, and when you found great crevices in the earth and laid down in them at night, symbolically to be born again in the morning. These things have been known, but because you have moved so far from the naturalness of your world, they are deeply embedded in your consciousness and not easily accessible to you for your daily use. One way to view an Enlightened One is to see them as someone who has activated and understood all of the symbols in their *earthbound* psyche. All of your symbols do not have to be activated for you to be enlightened, but the ones connected to the earth plane can be, when that is your goal. Let us then activate as many of these as we can, so you can take them into your life and begin to work with them in a meaningful way.

To do this, we will observe the naturalness of your world. Nature is one of the most direct mirrors and accessible teachers of your awareness. Nature and natural events speak to places inside of you the mind cannot reach. Many of these symbols of nature are found in the *I Ching*, so this text serves as a guidebook to symbols. Five of these symbols we shall dwell upon this morning are found in this book. They are: *the mountain, the lake, the sun, dragon, and fire.* Let us look at how these symbols relate to the human condition.

First, mountain. Mountain symbolizes stillness, power, and endurance, qualities you associate with inner peace and centeredness. Lake is that still space within you which mirrors the unconscious as well as the Divine. When you look deeply into your own lake, you will see those emotions that bind you. The circle of the sun is the great symbol of Light, hope, and the awakening consciousness. It is the dispenser of darkness and fills you with feelings of warmth and safety. That mythological beast, the dragon, has been a symbol in the human psyche for thousands of years. Its fiery breath has been symbolized as lightning, the bridge between heaven and earth. Align yourself with the flight of the dragon and you will be able to discover those ideas, habits, and beliefs that have held you earthbound. And finally fire, the symbol of transformation and change. So let us now begin our meditations on these symbols and see how best they may be put to use in your life.

Meditation on Symbols from the *I Ching*
MOUNTAIN

In the days of old, when these symbols were put into words in the **I Ching***, the mountain was identified as 'Keeping Still.' You will begin this process of knowing yourself to be the mountain,*

104

'Keeping Still,' by feeling the attributes of mountain. Allow yourself to participate in mountainness. You are not separate from the earth. You **are** the mountain.

So then, gently close your eyes. Pull all your awareness from around you deeply into the body. Feel yourself solidly in your body. Become conscious of yourself seated on the floor or in the chair. Feel yourself as present in the body, and then begin to dwell on the idea of how you would feel if you were the mountain. How does the mountain feel itself? Allow yourself to feel the deep, vast power of mountain. Allow yourself to feel the strong, rock-like, powerful, enduring, quiet, patience of mountain. Allow yourself to feel the strength of mountain, of how mountain allows all things to happen around it, upon it, but remains mountain. Allow yourself to feel the peaks of the mountain thrusting up into the vault of the sky above. Feel those high, strong, brilliant peaks of power. Abide as the mountain, centered, grounded, and powerful. Pause.

If you continue to practice this exercise, you will find there is a strong, grounded, peaceful quality of endurance that is the essence of mountain, and as you develop these qualities, you can, in times of need, turn to the remembrance of mountain and reconnect with this experience. There is nothing outside of yourself that is not also within, and you contain the endurance, the patience, and the power of the mountain.

LAKE

Within the deep recesses of mountain lies the lake. The lake and the mountain are one, and they are within you. This lake can be imagined by you, so still feeling the awesome presence of mountain, move around the mountain body until you find the place where the lake within you is located. The lake, throughout mankind's history, is recorded as the mirror of the heavens. This lake within you will contain deep images, so upon locating it, **feel the lake within you** and see it clearly with your awareness. Make it deep. Make it full. Be aware of the color. Feel its warmth or coolness. Then feel yourself dropping down into the lake and begin to experience the images stored there. This is your lake. This is a mir-

105

ror of you. What are **your** depths? How does it feel to be in the stillness of this lake, to be in the deep, mysterious, so-called unconscious part of your being? There is nothing to fear here. Deep within you lies the mirror of the Divine.

Pause.

When you allow yourself to consistently fall, drop, or move into the depths of your being, into your lake, and remain there with alive consciousness, you will begin to receive impressions from this lake of the unconscious—symbols, words, thoughts, ideas, questions and answers. For those of you who are interested in understanding the unconscious and do not have a way of access, I recommend that you practice this day after day, so the deep, dark, mysterious, and often fearful reaches of what you call the unconscious will become safe and familiar—a friend and not the enemy—something to be welcomed and not something to be avoided. By this simple willingness to submerge yourself into this lake within, you will begin to 'know thyself,' and no greater gift can you give to yourself than this.

SUN

There is mountain and there is a lake within the mountain. Now we add the symbol of the sun. As you sit as mountain with lake within, bring into your consciousness the awareness of sun rising over the horizon and falling on the face of the mountain. Experience it ablaze on the horizon, and feel it as it warms all of the crevices, the ravines, the valleys and the peaks of you as mountain. Feel the sun warming you, touching you, caressing you, filling you with fire, filling you with light, warmth, comfort, and safety. One of the most powerful, yet simple, sun meditations the earth has ever known is as follows: Each morning, when the sun awakens, greet it as it rises up out of the darkness and fills the landscape. Feel it on your face, arms, torso, and feet. Stand there and simply experience the rising of the sun. This meditation is as old as man. You do not have to live in an open countryside to make this meaningful. When the sun reaches your place of living, awaken and sit quietly, facing the direction of the rising sun, whether you can see it or not. Imagine the sun's rays racing from the horizon towards you, and as it lights up your mountain, feel what its warmth stirs in you.

This image has the ability to stir deep feelings of gratitude within you. Day after day, remember that the light comes and fills you, that it burrows its way into all of the crevices of your being, of your body, emotions, and mind, burning away the shadows of the dark, of the night, leaving you warm, clear, safe, filled, and comforted. What feelings does this stimulate? What remembrances? This is the moment to acknowledge, with deep gratitude, the Light symbolized by the sun. In endless cultures of the world, the sun is the symbol of God. It is the remembrance of God coming once again to you, permeating you and caressing you, reminding you that, without your doing anything except turning your face to it, the Light of God embraces and fills you.

Pause until you feel a completion.

Earth Plane Mandala

To pull these symbols of mountain, lake, and sun into a powerful reality so that their attributes are a conscious part of you, we will use the process of creating a mandala.

Sit quietly with your circle empty and waiting before you. Reflect on each of these symbols, one by one. Reflect on them in your awareness, all that we have just discussed, all that we have just experienced. Then softly gaze at your collection of colors, intuitively choose one and hold it in your hand. Now, with your deepest wish that the essence of mountain reveal itself in some way on your paper, with eyes softly gazing, simply move your crayon or your chalk gently over the surface of the paper, allowing mountain to move through you. Then, without any analysis of what you have done, still with a soft gaze, select a color or colors for lake and do the same. Simply allow lake to flow through you onto paper. If you go outside the confines of the circle, it does not matter. If you feel prompted to add another color, do so, but all of this with eyes softly gazing. Again, selecting the color or colors that represent the sun, and using the same process as above, allow the feeling of sun to create itself on your paper. These mandalas are not meant to be works of art. They are meant to be motions of your being responding to your connection with the wondrous natural world. The world of nature is always ready to stand as a symbol of the wholeness of things, to remind you that all the energies on this wondrous planet play through each other, support each other, nourish each other, and reveal one part to the other.

Pause until finished.

DRAGON

For this exercise you will need a notebook and pen or pencil.

The **I Ching** makes intimate use of the symbol of the dragon. It does this in various ways, but for today let us choose one and put it in our own words. Holding the truth that energy follows thought, we are going to use the dragon to teach us what things are holding us earthbound, and how it feels to fly free of earthbound ideas. Start with as much reality as you can to visualize a dragon, one large enough to be powerful, but not large enough to frighten you. Place yourself carefully, securely, upon its back. This is not a fantasy, but imagery which, if used correctly, can teach you a great deal. Now feel the spread of the dragon's wings beneath you, feel its motion as it begins its first attempts to pull free of the earth. In those first few moments, you will become aware of a certain resistance, a certain inability to perform the liftoff. So with your pencil and paper in hand and your eyes closed, feeling the powerful stroke of the wings and the resistance of the earth, write down those things that come to mind from which this resistance might be made. Be both specific and general. For example: Fear, general. Fear of death, specific. Fear of sin, fear of guilt, specific. Desire, general. Desire not to leave your children, specific. Anger, general. Anger at X for x, anger at B for b, specific. Keep writing until you feel that moment when the sweeps of the dragon's wings pull away from the earth in free flight.

Short pause.

Now, my friends, be aware that your **psyche** has the capability of expanding into higher realms of consciousness. This is the kind of movement that you can now expect to feel. At this point you can either stay in flight with your dragon or allow the mental

108

form of dragon to fall away and follow your consciousness up higher and farther, and higher and farther, until you actually feel a part of your consciousness is beginning to fill the heavens. Spend as much time as you can feeling that expansion, that vast pervasive consciousness. Stay out in the vastness as long as possible.

Pause.

When you feel yourself drifting back down toward the earth, follow the pull in a graceful curve, with gentleness and gratitude, knowing what you have done once, you can do again. Having experienced this flight once, you can experience it whenever you choose to.

The final part of this exercise is to then carefully record the thoughts, feelings, promptings, or urges that might occur to you as a result of your journey, just as one who journeys around the earth plane records the happenings of the day. And if there is a sense of having let go of any of those resistances that made your take-off difficult, record this victory also.

Pause until completed.

FIRE

Perhaps one of the most mysterious symbols in the psyche is that of fire. When you consider the history of man, you will see, with the discovery of fire, man's journey took on a totally new dimension. Fire is a symbol of transformation, but it also depends on something outside of itself for existence. It must cling closely to something else in order to burn. This is why in the *I Ching* it is called 'The Clinging.' 'Clinging' has come to mean something negative in your minds. In the present day, you feel you must cling to nothing, yet if you didn't hold tightly to that which you wish to change, and examine it with awareness, how would you bring about those transformations of the psyche that you need? The clinging, the brightening, these are words for fire. When fire moves from one object to another, it leaves behind transformation of all kinds.

As a symbol of change, what then does fire mean for you? We are assuming there are certain parts of your psyche, your life, and your inner and outer world you would like to transform in *some way. You can do this by reidentifying, remodeling, and recreating those things you would like to change.*

It is very difficult, if not impossible, to make any change until you are aware of what it is you wish to change, so this is your opportunity. Using your notebook and pencil once again, sit quietly, and turning your attention inward, begin a gentle, yet exacting list of those things you would like to change.
Pause.

*For the second part of this exercise, you will need a partner. It is my contention you all **know** how you can truly transform, reshape, and recreate those things you just listed. With a partner, select one thing from your list and ask the other person what **they** would do, how **they** would begin to work on your problem. When you have finished, have your partner select one of theirs. With a fresh point of view, you now have an additional tool to help you solve those dilemmas.*

Pause until completed.

Transformation is the process of taking something old and changing it into something more to your liking, perhaps more beautiful, more meaningful, or more useful. I would like to take a moment now to speak about the fiery transformation of anger. Some of you are so cool that you have no fire, because you equate fire with anger and have found anger to be unacceptable. But what you must realize is the fire of anger can also kindle the fire of the Soul. People form icy barriers around themselves when they are trying to keep other people, pain, or difficult emotions away. All of that iciness begins to melt when anger is present. Fire can break up old patterns in a very direct way, especially when it is the fire of the Soul rising up to say, "It is time to transform."

Fire is the element that you fear most because fire can burn out of control. It has made a difference since it came to this planet and it will make a difference until the end of this planet. Out of control, fire is the most destructive symbol on earth. Yet when we use its transformative power, fire has the ability to bring us Home. An Enlightened Being is one whose heart is on fire, whose eyes flash with an inner fire. What does that mean? Let us dwell on the

110

image of fire in the mountain as our last meditation.

Transformation of Anger — A Meditation

*The **I Ching** uses fire in the mountain as a compelling image. With this before us, let us again go back to your feeling of yourself as the mountain. This time, instead of the coolness of the inner lake, we are going to bring in the heat of fire.*

*Sitting as mountain, begin to form in your mind, and then into a feeling (and this feeling is important), the remembrance of an event that greatly angered you. Take a few moments to recreate the event and to allow yourself to experience it in the solar plexus area. As it builds, you will become aware of a feeling which could be called heat. Investigate it carefully. Is it dull or sharp, sullen or bright? Does it burn fitfully or steadily? Now, making no effort to change these feelings, create an incredibly beautiful fire burning in the same area. Allow this greater, blazing fire to **totally embrace and consume** the other, earlier feeling. Feel the heat of this new, clean, Divine Fire. See the colors of red and blue, orange and yellow. Hear the roar and crackle of Divine flames. Sit there quietly, allowing them to fill you with a new cleansing kind of a feeling. Let this fire build to as great an intensity as you need to until you **feel** those smaller fires of anger have turned to ash. This is a technique you can use to burn up past angers or help you as an 'on the spot' technique for consuming anger at any time. Please remember, it is essential to **allow yourself to feel the new anger as it builds and then to call in the Divine Fire to burn it**. Increase this Divine fire until you truly feel the transformation. Do not stop until the original feelings have indeed turned to ashes. This is possible!*

Pause until completed.

Fire has always been the symbol of transformation of mundane, earthbound material into the formless, limitless expansion of the Divine. Energy follows thought, my friends. The more you dwell on the creation of the Divine Fire in your heart, the sooner you will finish your transformational process. Please, do not discard this technique until you have tried it, because it could change your life.

111

ALLIES

Symbols brought into the physically observable, like that of the ally (animal guide), can be dynamically helpful. Native Americans have lived long and successfully with the wisdom and guidance they have found anchored in the animal kingdom. Even their names, like Sitting Bull, Black Hawk, and White Buffalo Woman, testify to their intimate relationship with the animals. Other traditions such as the vision quest and sweat lodge praise and respect the spirit wisdom of the natural.

Bartholomew repeatedly utilizes the different ways in which we can benefit from the world around us. From the kingdom of the natural, 'he' offers the guidance of our animal teachers. For when asked, these animals can relfect our own inner knowingness and the courage to align ourselves with this wisdom. —Ed.

Before we go into a detailed discussion of allies and how to use them in your life, I would like to say a few things about the wonder of the animal kingdom—not only the human kingdom, but the kingdom of the winged ones, the finned ones, the four leggeds. These kingdoms have been doing an amazingly wondrous job on behalf of the planet from the earliest days until now, and a part of that experience is still deeply embedded in the consciousness of the earth. I would like to bring out certain strands of it now for your re-remembering. None of this material should seem very new to you, as it is, after all, a record of your own journey and therefore a part of your own awareness.

So, let us go back to the days when man was first attempting to solidly anchor himself onto the earth plane in the physical forms that are now called human bodies. At the same time, there were, in the mountains, the rivers, the valleys, the seas, vortexes of energy that man was able to connect with at any time. These vortexes of energy are now called animals, fishes, and birds. In those early days they were powerful helpers, and all of the different parts of nature worked together in order to unify what was to become the earth plane experience. Man, by simply turning his thoughts toward those energy fields, was able to receive very specific help and guidance.

For example, let us say a tribe of men moving across the open plains was looking for water. In those days, it was not difficult to find because they simply attuned themselves to the winged ones and the answer was forthcoming. When they were looking for foodstuffs, the answer was simply to attune to the world of animal consciousness and ask. And so it was, the animal kingdom consistently being able to help, to give man the assurance that all was well. Mankind, in turn, played its role in the grounding of animal consciousness. A tremendous bond of reciprocal love, admiration, and gratitude was born.

To this day, it is a hallmark of an old soul to have a deep love, and often a deep rapport, with other kingdoms. Many people who are spiritually alive and awakened have reentered the realm of deep communication with these friends and companions. It is clearly an attribute to be able to bridge the seeming gap between the different lines of world creation. And I feel the time to do that is now, and many of you are ready to begin to deepen this communion. I would like to point out a few reasons as to why such a deepening might be helpful for you.

It is a true statement that one of the manifestations of the New Age is a yearning to break down the barriers between the different worlds, namely the seen and unseen worlds, and the barriers between all of the life forms on this planet. By attempting to commune with, understand, and become alive to the truths of an animal ally, you will have done a great service for yourself and the planet. In breaking down the barriers and building a bridge of communion, you can create a path for others to follow. Each time you truly communicate with some form other than your own kind, you are bringing a wondrous power forward on the earth plane. The entire planet is moving toward Oneness, a Oneness when all the different forms of life will be able to once again share and aid each other's evolution. It is a beautiful thought, is it not, to be able to understand the wisdom of a 5,000 year old tree, to blend your consciousness with the whales, to share the flight of the birds? It is a beautiful thought to be guided once again by a sense of wholeness rather than a sense of separation.

The subject of allies is very vast and obviously cannot be covered in this short a section. So I would simply like to share various truths about allies, of which this is not meant to be a total statement.

Some of the places you can most easily find access to the

114

usefulness of allies are in the stories, myths, and fantasies of the different cultures of the world. They often contain the motif of an animal, bird, or fish that appears in order to help man. It usually comes to help the hero or heroine get out of some difficulty, or find his or her way when lost, or simply to bring a teaching or warning. A study of these stories, often called fairy tales, can give a sense of how man has used this help. In the beginning, when these tales were written, there was the knowledge that truth was contained in them. But as the centuries progressed and man became more sophisticated, these truths have moved into the realm of imaginings. If you re-examine and pay attention to the lessons of these great stories, you can discover how their wisdom can be used by you in your own life.

In this section we will be presenting a technique on how to find your ally. I ask you not to rely solely on this one meditation, but to look within yourself to find new ways of connecting with them. Some of you will find, for example, that you already have an affinity for an ally, whether you are conscious of it or not. This can be observed in your outer life. Some of you collect feathers, statues, or other works of art symbolizing the animal kingdom without knowing why. Having done this on an unconscious level, perhaps it is time now to become conscious of what you have drawn to you. What kinds of pictures do you have on your walls? Pay attention and you will find them to be indications of the presence of a friend who is waiting for you. Other people may send you a statue or poster of an animal without quite knowing why. Be alive to these indications, please, and see if there is not some kind of pattern or some kind of constancy here.

It is important to remember, my friends, that your ally changes as the years go on. As you become more integrated and make good use of your current ally, it can open up possibilities for you to move on to another animal teacher. Everything outside of you, if looked at deeply, has something to say to you, and many of you are ready to be the listener, observer, and student, rather than the teacher. Once you become alive to the idea that all of the createdness has a deep yearning to commune and blend with you, every moment becomes alive. Going for a walk, whether it be on a busy street, in the forest, or by the seashore, becomes an exciting event, far past just the delight of the physical.

Deep within the ancient lore of your planet, there have always been those wise ones, called by different names in different traditions, who had the ability to read the signs of the physical world. Some were called shamans, some magicians, some wise old men, some medicine women. Whatever the name, these wise and evolved ones were known to have the ability to read the outer world and tell you personally what the message would be. Although these great ones are few and far between in this period of man's destiny, you all have within yourselves the ability to be a shaman unto yourself. What is required is something very simple. It is the ability to drop to that place within you that yearns to truly hear, see, and understand; to open to the desire for wisdom and ask whatever your gaze rests upon to teach you, caress you, or simply blend its energy with yours.

I have told you often, and you know it to be true, that on the deepest level *all* of the createdness is connected. It is out of this basic truth that one energy form has the ability to blend with and sense the deep validity, beauty, and wisdom of another. It is my belief you will greatly enhance the wonder of your own life if you would each begin to blend in this way, day by day.

The things that your ally can do for you are numerous. Here are but a few of them. When you meditate deeply on your ally, you can feel where you are strong, where you are weak, and why this ally has been given to you. The ally comes to show you ways to strengthen yourself and to remind you of attributes about yourself you have forgotten. The ally also delights in playing with you, in bringing out the part of you that is not so intense, not buried in fear. This is an essential attribute of the ally. So, when you meditate upon the ally, imagine what it would be like to be playful in relationship to this great friend. Allow your imagination and inner memory to combine in flights of delightful fantasy. Feel, for instance, what it would feel like to be so close to a great black bear you could tumble in the meadows with it.

The ally also comes to transport you to a new destination. In

116

many fairy tales and myths, the human either mounts or attaches himself to the ally, or, in some cases, is swallowed by the ally and taken to its destination. When you are in a meditative state with your ally, please do this simple and delightful exercise. Place yourself securely upon it and ask it to carry you to wherever it feels you need to go, and when you reach your destination, ask it to accompany you on your journey of exploration. These are not unimportant imaginings. These are ways to be lifted up and transported in reality to new levels of consciousness. You know about Pegasus, about the dragonriders, about the great whale. All of these friends can show you the next level of awareness that you are approaching and aid you in arriving at that new level. This is one of the oldest techniques of man, to allow the great, powerful ally to transport you to your next destination in consciousness. I urge you to experiment. I do not think you will be sorry.

An ally is also a comforter. To those of you who have not attempted it, it would be hard to describe the real sense of safety that many humans have when they envision themselves being held in the arms of a great and powerful ally. Your myths talk about human children being raised by the animals. In truth, the wondrous heart of these allies is available for your comfort. I suggest you attempt this connection when you are feeling misunderstood, lonely, deprived, or isolated. If you are open to the experience, there is little doubt that you will be able to feel safer, less alone, and more peaceful than before.

An ally can strengthen you where you are weak. When you feel defeated and you know what is before you calls for a courageous action, yet you are afraid, simply spend a few moments experiencing the courage of your ally. Allow your mind to wander through the different choices available and let your heart select the one that represents to you courage in the face of your present adversity. Allow yourself to feel, to share that courage in a physical way. Feel yourself being filled with it. The animal kingdom is filled with wondrous powers. Their attributes of courage, resourcefulness, wisdom, empathy, devotion, and selfless service have been recorded throughout the centuries. I ask you to give deep consideration to expanding your being by finding an enduring relationship

117

with these parts of the One who stand ready to help you. Many of you feel close to specific animals, but your ally may be something quite different. So the first thing to do is *drop all expectations you might have about what your ally is.*

One of the reasons the other kingdoms are trying to reach you is because they know there is a loneliness that some of you experience. As you move through the natural world, as you walk in the woods or along the shore, there is a feeling of aloneness in the human. Other kingdoms do not feel it because they keep the interconnection between themselves. We will try now to reconnect so nourishment can pass back and forth between you. In feeling the fullness of it, you need never be concerned about isolation because you are in truth surrounded with an 'otherness' which is always trying to reach you. So take a seated meditation position and let us begin.

Ally Meditation

As you sit cross-legged, place your right hand on your right knee and your left hand on your left ankle. Now very gently rock back and forth, or side to side, whichever feels more comfortable. Allow your consciousness to sink into your body with this soft and gentle rocking. When your body is calm and your mind is quiet, come to center and rest.

Pause until people become still.

Your ally can be found either on the ground, underneath the sea, or in the sky. As we explore each of these areas, be aware of which one pulls on you the strongest.

First, the sea. Begin by feeling yourself walk across a sandy beach toward the sea and enter the water. Quietly and powerfully, you submerge and find yourself drifting through the vast, fluorescent blue-green depths to land on the ocean floor. Find a comfortable place to sit and, if this feels like home, remain. If it does not, follow me.

Short pause.

Return again to the beach, and this time, with powerful wings, spring into the sky. See yourself in its blue vault, above

118

and past the clouds. Open and vast it is, as you float free. Feel the power of the winds as they move. Feel yourself soaring easily with the wind. If this is your place, stay. If it is not, follow me.
Short pause.

Return again to the beach, and now feel yourself being projected deep into a forest. This forest is filled with the rich smell of the earth and the sounds of leaves rustling in the breeze. The sun slants through the trees, warming the earth below. Find yourself a comfortable, soft, embracing place and rest there.
Short pause.

As you rest in the safety of your natural home, either the sea, sky, or land, bring your awareness to your breath. As you sit, feel your breath rise and fall, rise and fall. Now, in the present, in this place, take your hands and cup them before you—eyes closed. When I say the word "look" I want you to look into your hands and tell yourself what animal you see. One, two, three, Look. Now, in whatever way is appropriate, close your eyes and hold this animal to your heart.
Pause.

When you have finished communicating with this animal, take out your paper and pencil and write down what you saw and felt. Underneath the name or description of your animal, make one list of its 'positive' attributes and one list of its 'negative' attributes. As you do, please use your connection with this animal to describe it, and do not go to a memory of what you have heard or learned about it.
Pause until finished.

The following are some examples of the different animals people found in this exercise: a smiling monkey's face; a tiny, tiny baby deer; a deer that turned into a tiger; a raven; the nose and face of a raccoon; the strong wings of a falcon; a cloud; a snake; a badger; a whale; a dolphin; an eagle; a winged horse. We have chosen the eagle to use as an example of the dialogue between one participant and Bartholomew. This participant was present for several ally workshops held over a span of two years. We have chosen this example so we can follow one person's process over a period of time. —Ed.

So you have found the eagle to be your ally. The challenge of anyone who has a strong power bird for an ally is to be able to soar on your own and understand that without that soaring you will not be content. At the same time, there is the need to put aside that loftiness when appropriate. It is very hard to snuggle up with a large, strong bird. You have to pull in your wings and temper your beak and claws, thereby becoming a softer manifestation of that same power.

Those of you who have powerful birds as allies are often people who have trouble with intimacy. Your difficulty is not with friendships, because you can make beautiful movements in the air with your friends, but in your intimate relationships. Until you learn how to fold your wings and become soft, you will frighten people, because they tend to see you soaring in distant and lofty states and not in your receptive, sharing aspect. Your job is to do the best you can to balance these two parts of your being. As the high-flying, independent one, you do the nurturing. You must understand, where you will meet and blend with others is when you allow yourselves to be nurtured. This is very important. Great birds can be frightening, but soft, yielding powers are magnificent. Keep reminding yourselves that it gives other people pleasure to nurture you. So what can you tell us about your ally, the eagle?

P: The attributes of my eagle are: free-soaring, strong, far-seeing, joyful, brave, beautiful, fierce, and powerful. If this bird were confined, it would lose control and it might kill itself trying to get free.

B: And what things do you find confining, my friend?

P: I hate to say this, but some relationships.

B: What aspect of relationship?

P: The loving, warm, soft part you were talking about.

B: Those things confine you?

P: They make me nervous.

B: Why do they make you nervous?

P: Because those are things I would really like to experience and I am afraid if I get them, I'll lose them. So I'm always trying to figure out how much is safe to allow.

120

B: Alright, is it possible what you are saying is you have difficulty allowing someone to nourish you? Are you afraid if you get this nourishment, that somehow it will be withdrawn? Is this the point? Or what is the real point?

P: It feels like I'll get addicted to nourishment and then it will be withdrawn and I'll be left powerless.

B: There is a wonderful thing about a bird. It can fly, it does not have to stay in one place all the time. Any intelligent bird, if it was no longer being nourished, would take to the air and find another to nourish it, and as the eagle can move about by choice, so can you! Now let us move on to the eagle's other attributes.

P: The difficult aspects are: it's dangerous; it's not trusting; it's wild; it's defensive; it's fiercely independent. If it was threatened, it would immediately attack. It's not a bird that would allow any kind of closeness.

B: Not at all? Not even to a select few?

P: The only closeness I can see is to its children.

B: How did it get these children?

P: It laid eggs?

B: And how did it occur to this eagle to lay an egg?

P: (Pause) It let another bird near it?

B: That's right—very, very near it indeed. Those of you who do have the high-flying birds such as eagles, geese, hawks, and vultures as allies will never have hordes of people around in an intimate situation. But what you will have is a few strong and equal allies close to you, and the rest of the people will be at a relative distance. But don't worry about it. It's simply the "nature of the beast" and it's wonderfully free.

P: What I would like to get rid of is the fear of loss. I would also like to get rid of the feelings of possession, jealousy, and neediness that go along with the desire for softness. At this point I realize that you can't cuddle an eagle. The thing that was missing was the softness and the love and the warmth.

B: You can't cuddle an eagle in flight, I will agree.

P: I couldn't even cuddle it in my arms. I mean, I could make it the right size, but I couldn't get past the fierceness. It was a very regal eagle.

B: Do you believe that there is something that is less than regal about closeness?

P: Yes.

B: Would you rethink that? The eagle would die as a species if it could not lay with softness and allow nourishment to come to it. I repeat, your challenge, my friend, is to balance between the fierce isolation and power of your independence and the harmonious movement to ground yourself in softness and allow others to nourish you. You will find there are a lot of people who will be willing to risk nourishing an eagle, but it takes someone with similar power. They may not *appear* to, but gentleness is a very strong power.

P: An eagle has vision and clarity. Wouldn't the clarity of its vision, that far-seeingness, get me past any feelings of smallness or fear I had? Wouldn't that be a balance?

B: My friend, whenever you are afraid of loss, would you just fly? Literally take your eagle and soar as high as you can. You described the power of this bird beautifully, so when you get into the place within you that feels fearful or weak, the anecdote is immediate: move to the part in your being the eagle represents and manifest its power in your psyche at once. Instead of staying in the feelings of weakness, move with deliberation, with sweet will, to those things you know give power to your flight. Do you understand what I am saying? All you have to do to pull in one of these powers is *move to it*. You don't have to create it. It's there. So move to it and fly!

A year later, the participant was in another ally workshop. After connecting with the ally, Bartholomew again asked for a list of attributes. —Ed.

P: My ally is still the eagle. The feeling was of flight, freedom, and just being high. It is the highest flying and furthest seeing bird. But this time I also had the feeling it is very protective of what it sees. It can observe what is going on, the movement of other animals and the river and forest. It is protective and it loves them all very much.

B: What is its job as protector, my friend?

P: To keep them safe.

B: How? There is one very particular way that an eagle could help. How, for example, could the vast and glorious, high-flying eagle help the small little rodent that runs along the valley floor?

P: By being there when something attacks it.

B: That is one way. And another?

P: It can tell it of approaching danger.

B: Exactly. Birds are the communicators. They are the ones who can take thoughts, ideas, and messages from one place to another. They fly high to see, and when they see things, there comes the responsibility of doing something about what they have seen. They feel compelled to help, to defend, to alert.

P: The eagle is not a light bird. I mean light in the sense of, say a sparrow that has a light body and quick movements. An eagle doesn't have that. It's a heavy bird.

B: You mean heavy in the colloquial sense?

P: Yes, serious. A serious bird. Even the joy it feels in flight is kind of fierce. It's sharp, and it's powerful. So again the difficulty is in lightening up. One of the ways the eagle can do that is to see what is going on with the other animals down below and take part in that for itself.

B: In what way?

P: To respond, for instance, to the playfulness of bear cubs—and to enjoy that.

B: Are you saying the eagle needs to look at what it sees and mirror, as part of itself, those aspects it feels it needs to?

P: Yes.

B: Wonderful!

P: It really doesn't fear anything except man. And the reason it fears man is because man is not confrontive. Man won't deal with it face-to-face. Man will kill it, trap it, snare it, or shoot it. Something that is done at a distance—not cleanly, not in any kind of face-to-face confrontation.

123

B: What does this say about your world? How then do you perceive people in your life? Which kinds of people do you get along best with?

P: I get along best with people who are honest about what is going on with them, how they are relating to me, and who will confront me on whatever is happening between us. I may not always like what I hear, but I prefer it.

B: And what enrages you?

P: A sense of falseness, of distance, of not being willing to face issues.

B: Not everyone will say this about themselves, because not everyone needs to confront. This is why we cannot make rules. The tendency of the bird clan, with all of its power, is to say, "Ah, this is how I perceive things, therefore the world should be thus." There are many people, my friend, who would be very uncomfortable in the stance of the eagle because it is not their way. I think the bird clan needs to understand that, along with the ability to see many things, comes the inclination toward being 'above it all.' And out of that can come arrogance. So keep this in your awareness, my friend, when you are off soaring above the earth. But enjoy the flight.

MYTHS

Another symbol-rich source
for self-exploration is the
myth. "The Greek word for
myth is 'mythologia,'
meaning the collective
dreams of humanity. The
motif one traces of any
people will be the same as
the motif in the dreams of
other people. It is a human
dream; it is vast, it is
beautiful. A myth is a
road map to the
extraconscious."[1] Going
to your own inner
story, inviting it out in
either the spoken or
the written word, is a
startling experience. Listen
deeply to yourself, with no
judgment, and you will be
dazzled and moved by your
own inner truth. So let us
now set the stage for an
experience with our own
creative myth.

[1] *Justin Moore, June 1986 Dream Workshop, Taos, New Mexico.*

It is summer, the first day of the Ally workshop in Taos. We are in a small, aspen-filled canyon east of town. A sparkling stream runs by, meadowlarks are singing, sunshine and cool breezes create shadows and keep everything in motion. We have just come back from our lunch break, comfortably filled with food and our surroundings. Bartholomew clears 'his' throat and begins. —Ed.

So then, good afternoon. There is a tendency in the human to develop in the course of their lifetime what could be called a 'thick skin.' This is an interesting concept arising out of the feeling that you are tired of being hurt by 'life,' so therefore you will no longer let 'life' into you. But the price you pay for keeping out pain is high, for at the same time, your life goes dead and you can no longer feel the bliss of it. In the end, you find you have lost the feeling of power, wonder, and direction that your life has had. Myths can help activate, remind, rejuvenate, and bring such experiences back. They can empower you to such an extent that you will begin again to allow life to flow through you.

There is written deeply within each of you a wondrous myth that is your own. It is the story of your struggle toward consciousness. It is filled with your own personal journey, encompassing both the successes and failures, the tears and laughter, the expansions and contractions of your life. This myth does not look or sound the way your so-called human life has. It is of a totally different order of consciousness. It has very little to do with the path your physical body has walked. Your life on the physical plane, your actions, and your experiences, are really only a small part of what is occurring as your life unfolds.

There are deep, vast, wondrous parts of your being participating in creation on levels of consciousness that cannot be viewed by the human eye or felt by the human hand. These vast sweeps of expansion and understanding are going on simultaneously as you move through your human experience. These other parts of your being encompass such areas as the dream world, fantasy world, intuitive world, and more. You are a multi-dimensional being, only one small part of which is projected into an earth body living an earth life. So when you enter the realm of myth, most especially your own myth, turn within and discover your own story. And as you write or speak it, this story will begin to touch you with its reality so you will know you are bringing into your consciousness wondrous lessons that different parts of your being have already participated in. This story or myth comes, not as an imagining, but as another tool to enliven your awareness.

It is easy to believe you are nothing more than a body with an assortment of emotions, thoughts, and responses, moving in a linear manner through a chaotic world where fear is on every side. If you allow yourself to write your own myth, you can experience directly the strength and wisdom of your own teaching. You would be calling on those parts of your own being that have access to those realms in which lie help, encouragement, warning, and inspiration. You would *know* the struggles of your mythological hero, heroine, or creature are your story. And through this process, new ideas, solutions, and possibilities will be presented to you.

There is a part of you constantly creating the next events of your life. By using your own personal myth, you participate more closely in that process. For example, you might find as you create another chapter of your myth in the morning, that later in the day, re-enactment of those events might appear in your life. You might find yourself acting in accordance with what you created on your page that morning. You might find yourself facing an old situation that you can now respond to in a totally new way, because your hero or heroine, being faced with a similar one, found an alternative solution you can participate in.

Let us assume at this moment, each of you has some kind of unresolved difficulty in your life, and you have tried to change this situation but met with no success. For example, let us assume the difficulty is in relationship, that one of your relationships has become bogged down in repetitious patterns of attack and counter-attack. No resolution has come to mind. May I suggest, in the

128

quiet of the early morning or in the darkness of the night, you take your pad and pencil and begin to create a story which is not a mirror of the relationship, but with the relationship in your consciousness. Begin to write a myth about a central character, what happens to them, and what resolutions and victories are achieved. You can resolve conflicts by using this technique of personal myth creation, as you bring into the limitation of the old a new creativity with vaster sight and deeper understanding. Instead of going through the endless dialogue between you and other, with you trying to win and them trying not to lose, just abandon the field entirely and expand into that realm where the solution lies and simply bring it through in the form of a myth. These stories do not have to be long. They simply provide you with the opportunity to turn to another part of your consciousness and bring through some practical information.

There is a part of the human consciousness, in its *collective* form, that is available to you. There are only so many dramas the human can live through and they are common to all of mankind. These dilemmas have been solved countless times by countless people. The knowledge of those victories is available to you because you are a part of the Whole, with access to all the wisdom that the Whole has ever created. The following exercise is one of many techniques that can make part of mankind's wisdom available to you now, in this moment of time-space when you need it.

Creating Your Own Myth

So, let us begin the practice of myth-creation. The suggestions are simple. Sit quietly, eyes closed, feeling the rising and falling of your breath within the body. Allow your thoughts to drain away into the ground below you. Simply sit and feel the breath rising and falling, and the rest of you in a state of quietness. Then, without thought, without planning, pick up your pen and begin with, **"The hero's (or the heroine's) name was . . . . ,"** *and then you fill it in. It doesn't need to be your name. Then you go on.* **"He awoke (she awoke) to find that he (she) was seated in . . . ."** *(a room, a valley, a castle, a car, a spaceship, on a bird, riding an elephant, whatever).* **When he (she) opened his (her)** *eyes, he (she) saw before him (her) . . . ." (whatever comes to your consciousness). Just move through these occurrences without thought. Some obvious things to consider including are: physical location; people present, if any; what the terrain looks like; animals; any sounds present; and most important, what the hero or heroine is feeling. "He (she) found himself (herself) in a state of pain. The pain was because . . . ." Associate yourself with the feelings they are experiencing and simply allow the myth to write itself. Do not start by saying you cannot do this exercise. These writings are not for publication, they are for emancipation. All of you speak, therefore all of you can write. Writing is nothing more than speech on paper. Travel as the hero or heroine from one event to another, spontaneously allowing all kinds of unexpected experiences, people, and manifestations to occur. This is the realm of imagination, magic, and creative power. So allow yourself to create, with magic and power, miraculous events, miraculous flashes of understanding, miraculous openings of mind and heart. Be willing to create a magical myth. It is through avenues like myth-making that you allow your human consciousness to remember there are always miracles, and life itself is the biggest miracle.*

We continue to follow our original workshop participant as they utilize their ally to tell their own myth. The myth was presented in writing a year later, so we now submit it in that form. —Ed.

MYTH: Lord of the Wind

The Lord of the Wind was born unconscious of himself during a storm that shook his egg from its nest and flung it from the tallest tree on the highest cliff downwind to the valley floor. It landed with a splash in the stream below, and was carried to a sandy spot on a small finger of land that pressed itself into the water. There, when the storm was at its height, with cracking thunder, amid streaks of pale lightning, the egg broke open. The soaked, scared occupant blinked and blinked again, looking for shelter. The lightning hurt his eyes and the thunder drove him up an embankment, where he tumbled into a sweet smelling nest of grass under an overhanging protective bush. He at once fell to

130

sleep.

Upon awakening, he found himself beak to bill with a large white duck, who had been politely demanding the origins, inclinations, and declarations of the present inhabitant of her nest. Scanning his short memory quickly, that same inhabitant admitted to not knowing much about any of those things. Though taken aback, the duck examined the newcomer minutely and finally reported him unknown to her. His nose was much too sharp, his feet much too large, and his eye much too piercing to be familiar or even comfortable. Thus closing the subject, the duck returned to the stream, waddled in, and paddled away. The small creature was left alone to ponder this news. It was disheartening to realize how lonely he felt and how difficult it was going to be, discovering who he was.

Taking heart from the warmth of the sun and the music of the stream, the creature made his way awkwardly back to the shore. Drinking deeply of the water, he felt strong enough to set out on his journey. He started upstream, stumbling often. Looking down at his feet, he saw them to be large, with sharp talons. They were definitely not made for swimming and not much better for walking.

He moved slowly and was concentrating intently on keeping his balance when he heard a loud shout, and a young aspen came crashing down before him. A stout beaver brushed past and began gnawing busily at the closest branches. Hiding his feet and presenting what he hoped to be a kindly eye, the creature inquired as politely as possible if perhaps the beaver might know or recognize him. Pausing briefly, the beaver gave him a quick glance, remarking on the strength of his front teeth, but the absolute uselessness of his front paws. No, he wasn't a beaver or any other forest dweller he had ever seen. Looking down at the small fuzzy stumps that hung by his sides, the creature realized with a sigh how right the beaver was. With them he could not pick up or hold anything, and he was at a loss to think of what they could be useful for. Thanking the beaver, he continued on his way.

And so it went. Time passed and the seasons changed and changed again as the creature wandered and searched. He, too,

131

had changed. His eyes were clear, his gaze steady. His feet were no longer too large for his body, which was now strong and covered with golden brown feathers. The fuzzy stumps were no longer fuzzy, but had also grown and reached down to trail along the ground as he moved. He had learned to walk without tripping over them, and at night he pulled them up over his back to keep himself warm when it grew cold.

The country had also changed. As he worked his way south, forest and meadow had given way to open grassland, studded with small, gnarled trees. Mesas thrust themselves up from the red, rocky earth and the sky was a brilliant, intense blue that held an ever-changing movement of clouds. The wind became his friend and constant companion. Sometimes it would whisper, sometimes it would shout at him. But always, when he turned his attention to the wind, it would bring him peace.

The creature had become resigned in his search, but also more firm in his resolve. He met many animals during his journey. Some had laughed, some had shown him kindness, and some had whispered their discouragement. He had seen it all, and in return was courteous and gave what help where he could. His pain and loneliness he kept to himself and he never stayed long in any place. His determination strengthened in his heart the farther he traveled, and he came to enjoy his life with a bittersweet acceptance of all it was.

So it happened that, on the third anniversary of his birth, the creature once again found himself looking for shelter from a gathering storm. The sky blackened and boiled. The wind shrieked, driving rain in flat sheets against the high, open mesa the creature was trapped upon. The only shelter he could find was a slight depression in the rocky ground, not far from the edge of the cliff. He settled himself in as best he could, and folding his stumps over his back for protection, he prepared to wait out the storm. The air grew colder and the rain turned to sleet, reflecting back the blue-white bolts of lightning that struck all around him. The creature was freezing, what breath he could manage, a pain to swallow. His eyes were frozen shut and he was filled with a great sadness. He felt the end upon him, and the death of his quest. He

132

lifted his head once more to say farewell to his friend the wind, and as he did there was such a crack of thunder and white-hot lightning that he was stunned and deafened. In an instant, the wind lifted him from his hiding place and swept him off the cliff. Such was the fury of the storm that he rose instead of fell. His struggles were useless and, with a last cry, he gave up the fight. Exhausted beyond endurance, the creature rose higher among the black clouds. Bursting through their tops, he was flung into another world.

Here was silence as deep as eternity, and light as brilliant as burnished gold against a sky of deep blue. The creature's heart burst with the beauty of it and he paid no attention to his body or his pain. The wind turned him over with a sigh and suddenly the useless stumps he had been dragging beside him snapped open, and he was soaring, suspended between his own strong, golden wings. Then the wind sang to him of their beginning, and in a moment of perfect joy, he knew who he was. He was known as Aquila,[2] but he was Lord of the Wind.

The rest of that day he spent soaring, wheeling and plummeting through the golden sky. By sunset he knew all there was to know about his wings, so he dropped through the clouds and found himself above the valley of his birth. As he glided in perfect flight over his valley, he called to each animal by name. He had known them all and they came at the sound of his voice, to gaze in wonder at the newly born Aquila. His heart was filled with Love as he took his place among them—Lord of the Wind.

B: Still an eagle?

P: Still an eagle.

B: And the qualities you've discovered this time?

P: Fierce, relentless, untiring, distant, alone, brave. To me the eagle represents freedom in its flight, it has clear vision, sees far, is a protector, it's loyal, a defender.

B: Are you describing yourself?

P: I hope so. I think so.

B: Can you sense an attribute that might be missing in what you have shared with us that you would like to have in this myth?

P: Not really.

B: I bring this forward because I think many of you share the same dilemma. You know how to suffer very well, but know little about how to live joyfully. The thing that I sense missing in the participant's myth is the incredible bliss of the whole process. It is necessary to bring out the bliss of the journey, the bliss of the flight, the bliss of it all. How can you include this in your narrative? What would your bird have to do or where would it have to go to get this quality?

P: The bird didn't know what it was. He didn't know until he was lifted off a cliff. He knew he was going to die and remembered all the animals he had met and how beautiful everything was. Then unconsciously he spread his wings and flew. He felt how easy it was and finally came to know himself. The animals also knew and every time he flew over them, they were also happy. What I learned through the myth is that grace and dignity come from the acceptance of all that is.

B: So the questions still remains—how?

P: He flew.

B: How?

P: He opened his wings and flew.

B: Right!

P: So the joy would come from the eagle realizing what it was, what it could do.

B: Right. What does that say about you? What are you to do?

P: To fly? To be what I was meant to be. *To do what would make me happy and in turn make those in my life happy.*

B: In your myth, was there anything basically different about the bird before and after it learned to fly? Was it the same bird? Was its birdness in any way changed by its flight?

P: Only its knowledge of what and who it was.

B: Exactly. Can you sense what I am driving at? Please think about it.

Each of you has a 'myth-maker' as part of your wholeness,

134

waiting to actively participate with you. To best use this friend, it should be called upon with a constant voice.

Each day, settled in silence, turn to it and ask your myth-maker to bring forth the next page or chapter of its truth, and to share with you its humor, love, clarity, and wisdom. If you do this on a regular basis, your myth-maker will become so alive and active its power will be ready for use at a moment's notice. A new vision of life will come into focus, leaving you stronger, vaster, clearer, and most of all, more alive!

[2]Aquila *is the Latin word for eagle.*

Part Four
QUESTIONS & ANSWERS

In 'his' work, Bartholomew at times will participate in
meetings which take the form of question and answer.
The following questions and answers come from such
sessions held in New York City, Detroit, and
Albuquerque over the past year and a half.
They have been selected for their general
interest in the areas of spirituality,
physicality, and in relationship.

quality

o we make mistakes?

I love the straightforwardness of the question. I could simply say no, but let's use an example to look at it from a wider perspective.

When you are going from one point to another in an airliner, it is rarely on course. The plane is always a little bit off and the pilot is constantly making adjustments. But in the end, it almost always lands precisely where it needs to. Please look upon your earth plane journey like that.

There are certain boundaries past which you cannot go. That, I think, is the issue. The deeper question which you are asking is: "Can you do just anything in your life?" No, you cannot. There *are* boundaries. Within those boundaries there takes place a certain movement, a certain motion, so you can have the delight of making adjustments within yourself just like the pilot. Please look at it this way—as adjustments rather than mistakes.

For example, you have difficulty with a friend and, as a result, lose the friend. Instead of bemoaning your loss, analyze the action that caused it. Be aware that you don't want to repeat it, and use it as a compass to bring yourself back on course. Then we can say there are no mistakes. You are constantly, delightfully moving from one event to another, experiencing them as you go, assured of reaching your destination. And you *will* reach your destination. You cannot miss. The trajectory is set. I tell you this with all the power of my knowing. The trajectory for going Home, back to the Source, has already been set. You cannot miss finding what you are looking for. Just continue to accept the fact there are adjustments which need to be made along the way. Make them with as much humor and as little humbug as possible.

Q: Would you expand on the understanding of boundaries?

I stated that you cannot go past certain boundaries. But please understand, your ego is not responsible for creating the boundaries in which you live your life. If it was, you would have killed each other off long before this. The ego gets angry and says, "I wish you were dead. Why don't you drop dead." But the ego does not set the boundaries, the Deep Self does. And the Deep Self knows the boundaries of the difficulties through which you have to move in order to keep on course. They differ from one person to another, which is what causes confusion. You want to have only one set of rules, thinking it is the rules that set the boundaries.

But the answer is an individual one. *You* know the boundaries within which you feel comfortable. For example, some people say it doesn't matter if you cheat on your income tax. And you might say, "Well, I don't know. It doesn't feel very good to me." But then again, you might receive a $10 bill in change from a hurried teller that should have been a $1 bill. And that you might accept. Do you understand? You have your own sense of boundary. You know you are hitting your boundaries when you begin to feel uncomfortable.

When you do something you don't feel comfortable with, you don't want to talk about it, and you don't want the world to see it. You don't want whoever it is that represents power in your life to know what you've done. These are the kinds of feelings that indicate you have hit one of your own boundaries. Use them to be responsible for analyzing the situation. See and know your own boundaries. It isn't hard. Just pay attention.

ow does one move from the statement, "I *believe* this is Truth to I *know* this is truth?" How does one go from *hoping* there is a God, hoping that life has a purpose, to *knowing* there is some kind of sense to it all?

It is a lifetime occupation to live the kind of life you are asking about. It takes a daily, ongoing commitment to having an open consciousness, so you know you are constantly receiving new material, *and* a constant watching for the old patterns that catch you up and limit you. I think the main solution is this: every day, in whatever way you can, be aware of what is going on in your own mind and in your own responses to the world.

If there is a God, then God is something you should be able to experience. God should not be something you read about on Sunday, but a *knowingness* always operating within you. God has to be there for you to experience and appreciate. But the human psyche says, "Well, if all that is true, why don't I *know* God is in me? Why don't I *know* I am alive with that kind of power?"

The answer is simple. Because there are so many earthly sounds ringing in your ears, you cannot hear the God within. You have been trained to move through your life with caution, to stay alert, so you can know what is taking place *outside* yourself. You do this in order to be safe. Now all of a sudden you must reverse the flow to understand what is going on inside. You must reverse the process. It is like being in a highly accelerated car that you begin to slow down. It takes awhile.

You do not live a spontaneous life, every day asking what it is you *need* and *want* to do, because your lives are planned days, weeks, months, and even years ahead. For example, one day you might awaken and feel you would like to shut out the world, stay home, be still, be centered. But you have made plans which are already in motion. So instead of staying with your spontaneous desire, you go. The spontaneous life means a simple life. It means keeping things as simple as you can within the parameters of the life you must lead. Since you do lead very active lives, you don't have to extend and compound your 'busyness' by becoming even

141

busier. You must have a willingness to live as simply as you can, whatever that means to you, in order to follow your intuitive responses. Every day, in whatever way seems appropriate, keep watching, keep listening for God. Keep alive to what you hope is going to happen.

In one form or another, hope and prayer are what helped the Enlightened Ones. They hoped and they prayed for many years, then one day they *knew*. They had crossed an arbitrary line they could not know was there. But it did not stop them. So, to live the Life Divine, you have to keep looking for it moment after moment. Some days you will look for it one way, some days another. Keep your consciousness alive to the possibility of experiencing God. That is what you want. Ask! "Is there a God? Is there not a God? Is this real? Is this false? Am I being told lies? Am I really in the hands of a Divine Power? What is truth?" If you really use that conscious desire to know, the way begins to open to the knowledge you seek. And that's really all that can be said.

Count on your own deep knowingness and trust there is something to find and that it is not 'made up.' *It is absolutely real*! Live the intuitive life. The closer you get, the quieter you are, the more alive you become, and the more the way shows you. There is no formula. There never has been, never can be. Just one day at a time. One foot at a time upon the path.

'm confused about the issue of safety, spontaneity, and living in the moment. My confusion stems from information given to me that has to do with the end of the year 1988. It suggests choices we could make now in preparation for that time, as dire things are predicted for the planet. So why does such information come to me? And why should I begin planning for 1988 when I can hardly deal with tomorrow?

Basically, the answer is very simple and you have already discovered it yourself. But let's just tell you what you've said. The only thing you can do in making decisions about the future is to stay in the present moment and ask, "In this moment, is it appropriate for me to be planning for 1988?" If the feeling is 'yes,' please go about it with as much love, zest, and humor as you can. If the feeling is 'no,' then don't. If you slip out of the moment, the mind will say maybe yes and maybe no. Then to further complicate the issue, you can ask other people for the answer. Some of them will say 'yes,' and some will say 'no.' So you are back where you started.

The deeper question is: What does mankind have to go on to decide, day by day, moment by moment, what is appropriate and what is not? You have *yourself* and that is all! It is your Self that you need to explore in order to discover what is maximum for *you* every moment. Make no mistake, what is maximum for you is maximum for everyone in your world. And to determine what that is, you must *examine your motives* and be honest in your examinations. Are you out for personal gain? Are you running away from a difficult life? A hard relationship? Or is your wish to create harmony, safety, and stability for as many people as you can? Please, do not judge yourself for those times that you choose personal gain, but *stand responsible* for those actions.

You believe there is a 'right way' to do things, but you also believe you are going through life blindfolded. What a terrible God it would be that blindfolds you, shoves you out into the world, and says, "Now you figure it out!" Since that is *not* the case, please acknowledge you didn't launch yourself onto this path without any tools. You don't go on an overnight camping trip without a great deal of paraphernalia, do you? You have big cars and trucks to take you where you want to go, and from there you carry everything on your back to your final destination. And that's for an overnight trip! So do you really think you would launch yourself into life without having the equipment to figure out where you are going? No! You are much wiser than that. Your deep intuition is one of your greatest 'pieces of equipment,' so use it! And please, don't worry. If it feels *appropriate*, if your motive is clear and it sounds exciting, then do it.

All you really have to go on is what you know inside yourself. And *it is enough*. Begin to trust yourself, otherwise you are locked into having other people be your authority. There is no authority other than your deep Self. I mean that. Look and you will know it.

've gotten stuck on one little phrase you have said, "Life is living you." Would you explain what that means?

You have the idea that you are a body running around a globe, and the globe is filled with chaos, with other people and events moving you around without your permission. This is the perception mankind has of itself and is locked into. So you have to be reminded, again and again, through verbal play, that you are simply being lived by an incredible energy vortex which is constantly moving through you. That energy we call 'Life.' If you thought about it deeply you would be less anxious, because in truth, you know you cannot, of yourself, give life to yourself. You know you cannot keep your heart beating and your breath going. You know, but you take these things for granted. You have forgotten how wonderful it is to be animated by a power, a God, an energy vortex that comes into you and moves you and has all of *your* life in It.

So, Life, or God, or the Divine, or the Light, is living you each moment. Where you get stuck is in the limited concept that somehow you have to keep *yourself* moving through life. My friend, if you would take yourself out of your thoughts and put yourself into *your own feeling process*, you would begin having wonderful experiences. God is not an idea and God is not a thought. *God is a feeling*. It wells up from within you and carries you from moment to moment.

The feeling of the Divine moves within you all the time. Keep asking it to manifest itself. Many of the Great Ones, before they awakened, went around begging for the God-Truth to reveal itself. It's the same process for you. If Life is living you, if there is a God present, then don't you want to feel it? Keep asking, and the more you turn your awareness upon this desire, the more it will become a reality for you. And I don't mean to just ask in moments when you are quiet or seated, I mean all the time, whenever you are doing what Life involves you in. And then *listen and watch for the response*.

If you are confused, it's because the mind chatters so loudly

145

you cannot listen and feel. So forget the mind and drop into antici-pation. Drop into yearning. Even drop into doubt and anger. Get out of your thoughts and into the feeling, because if you sit with *any* feeling long enough, the 'bottom' will fall out and you will begin to experience just *'feeling'* and that kind of feeling is God. If the Divine is real and if *one* human consciousness is capable of experiencing God-Consciousness, *why not everyone?*

The human body, exactly as it is, is an excellent receiver of Divine Power. So, please keep paying attention. Ask what it means: "Life is living me!" Ask it day after day, because the more you do, the more likely it is you will get an answer. And, my friend, if you don't ask, nothing will happen.

You have often told us that there are no rules. If there are no rules, by what standard then do I live my life?

From the time of your first coming to the earth plane, there was a part of you called the Deep Self that began recording, assessing, eliminating, and cherishing your experiences. As you have moved through all your lives, your 'Soul' has kept those true experiences that are in line with natural law. The rest rises and falls and moves away. Lifetime after lifetime, the things you have retained deeply within you are those you learned through your own experience were in line with Natural Order and Divine Law.

You do not have to be told when you are doing something harmonious with your inner law. You do not need to have a show of hands to realize that killing your neighbor isn't a good idea. There is a part in you that has recorded an amazing collection of '*right action*,' not because someone has told you, but because you have lived in 'wrong action' and found it to be inharmonious. The moment you realize this on the deepest level, 'wrong action' experience is set aside. *Right action becomes the standard by which you live your life*. You have been told you have lived, or are in the process of living, all aspects of human experience. When you hear this, you almost always identify with the 'negative' things, with the 'bad guy.' So I ask you to remember you have been the wonderful things, too. You have also been 'good guys.' Each time you moved through a life, you learned from it through a vast array of action. And you keep with you those experiences you can take anywhere in the createdness and have be harmonious.

When you leave a life to go to another area of consciousness, you cannot take anything that will in any way be harmful to another person or another consciousness. When you truly know that, you leave those experiences behind. What you take are the thoughts, feelings, and actions you have accumulated that were harmless. They may be small things, or very large ones, but through the centuries, I assure you, your accumulation has been great.

You know what harmonious right action feels like. You know it! You become confused when you look outside yourself, to other people to tell you what is 'right.' Please remember, you are not all at the same point in your learning processes. People act in negative ways in areas they have yet to understand. And others may have experienced the truth of things you do not yet know. So, do not judge. You do not know how to because you cannot see into the depths of another's being and know what is stored there.

You are all accumulating skills. So how do you learn the difference between rules and right action? You pay attention to your life. When some difficulty comes up for you, *stop and look* at it. Give yourself the time to make deep, inner decisions. Sit with the difficulty as it is, with the people as they are, with the whole situation as it is presenting itself.

Intuitively, the responses will begin to come. Out of these responses you will know which are harmless, which are harmonious with your own inner law. Then comes the hard part. Do you have the courage to act out of your inner response or do you not? This is the point of mastery.

Your inner nature has accumulated the most amazing and wonderful wisdom for you to draw upon. It is there, like a mirror, reflecting back the Divine part of your nature, which is not separate from the rest of you. If you simply drop into that Divine part and pay attention to the Deep Self, you will begin to see simplicity in your choices, and you will know what to do. It is not mysterious, my friends. The more complicated you make it, the farther you are from the spontaneous, direct answer.

ow can I feel at peace?

The only way I know for the human to feel 'at peace' is to have a deep inner sense that "God's in It's heaven and all's right with *my* world." It is a feeling that everything is in harmony each moment no matter how bad the situation looks. With this feeling comes the courage to do strange and wonderful things. When the discouragement committee rises up and says, "You can't do that," you find that you can. The warrior is born within you, and you find yourself daring new ideas to fill you, new roads to call you, new responses to delight you. *You feel new.*

There is a very deep desire in the human to have other people like you. No blame. Life goes easier if people like you. But an interesting thing will happen, my friends, if you dare to be the warrior and trust what comes to you. Either your friends will respond to your deepening awareness, or think you're totally crazy and have nothing more to do with you. And they leave your life. In either case, harmony and peace are yours.

But how to get this deep feeling of 'rightness?' Of peace? You begin as you do with any deep desire—by stating your intention. Tell yourself a hundred times a day, "I want *peace*. I want to feel it, *now*, within me. Nothing else matters as much. I don't need to be *right*, I don't need to be *heard*—I need peace. Now!" And then, withdrawing your awareness from the outer world, go inside to that place where peace abides and allow yourself to *feel it*! It is always there waiting for you to 'quicken' it into greater and greater waves of peaceful power. It's that simple. But you must go to that inner place again and again, leaving all other desires to quiet down and dissolve. You *can* do it if you want to badly enough.

Prayer has become a big part of my life. But there are lots of ways to pray and lots of people suggesting how to pray. Could you talk about prayer?

Number One: pray any way you can, whether you think you're doing it the right way or the wrong way. Just do it. Number Two: the goal of prayer is to pray without ceasing. It is to pray constantly in whatever way that appeals to you, so prayer becomes a part of your life.

Very simply, prayer is turning your consciousness within and starting up a higher vibration. The more you do it, the stronger the vibration. This is why I don't care *what* you pray for or *how* you pray. With the action of prayer, you build a vibration which increases, until there will come a time when you feel badly because an hour has gone by and you haven't in some way prayed. And soon you find that you need, more than anything, a way to live every moment *so that some part of you is always turning its face toward the Divine*—no matter whatever else may be happening. That's when you move into the realm of praying without ceasing.

Eventually, before the path ends, each one of you has to find a way to keep your face to the Divine, and prayer is certainly one way. So to answer your question, the only difference between 'good' prayer and 'bad' prayer is whether you're doing it in your heart or in your head. If you are doing it in your heart, you can feel the vibration being set up. If it's an automatic mental process, nothing very much happens. But there are no rules.

You want to do something you can 'feel' inside. That means getting *inside* of yourself and praying from there. You want a dialogue with the Divine your whole being responds to. And where you feel that is in the chest area—what you call the heart. Why do you think there are pictures of Jesus with His heart open and surrounded by Light? Because that is where the feeling was. Why are there pictures of the saints with their hearts aglow? Because that is where the feeling was. So, if you are going to expedite your prayer-learning, get into your heart and move from there. Prayer is not a mentalization or mindless repetition of someone else's words. If you *feel* your prayers, you *will* become alive to them.

My friend, you know clearly from your own experiences what ignites your heart and what doesn't. So I beg you to do those things. Without anybody's permission. I don't see any reason why you can't begin to feel that power getting stronger and stronger—until it floods your being and gives you a desire beyond all others, the desire to feel God all of the time.

Q: How can we pray constantly?

Just yearn for whatever you hold the Divine to be. Yearn for Its beauty, Its wholeness, Its power, Its wonder. *Yearn for It!* See these things in your mind and feel them in your heart as real and alive and filled with Light.

For some people, the discipline of formal prayer is absolutely maximum. For you, *feeling Life living you* is maximum. In the end, it is all the same. Prayer is done to increase vibrational frequency. When you are increasing vibrational frequency in other ways, you are doing the same thing as praying. You are feeling vaster, acknowledging it, being grateful for it, and living in an expanded state. Then you move into experiencing the *wonder* of that state, without the discipline. You move into the doing of it, just living life, feeling Life live you. Feeling Life live you *is* a form of prayer.

For you, it is appropriate just to trust the wonderful spontaneity of living. The test is whether or not you feel more love. If you feel more love, then whatever you are doing is right. Prayer in whatever form increases frequency. What was regimented and disciplined in order to get that frequency going, you did. Then one naturally moves to other parts of their being. And that's what you now do. So the next step is to blend both the discipline and the spontaneity.

The thing I ask you to remember is how necessary it is to find a way to be aware of the energy-in-motion all the time. If it's through prayer, do it. Whatever the method, allow yourself to feel it and be grateful. Please be grateful. You are all part of an experiment. There is something going on here, isn't there? The question is: What is it? What's happening? Pay attention to what is going on inside yourself. Whether it's through prayer or observation, whatever it is, just *be* there! Don't go on automatic. Live your life from a point of empowered awareness. It is delightful, and why not?

Life is never the same. You change all the time. You go from one room of your psyche to another and it's beautiful. I do not think you need worry. I think the more you enjoy your life, the more wonderful it is. Because the more you love, the more love will be around you. Less humbug and more wonder. And it's beautiful!

So, do not get stuck on rules. Praying without ceasing means finding the Divine in your life, watching yourself, and moving through life with gratitude and power. Be the 'observer' of your own process. There is an on-going, central 'I' that moves through your life. That is what you pay attention to. Sometimes it moves through prayer, sometimes through breathing, sometimes through sex, sometimes through walking. It moves through everything! Get in touch with the central 'knowing' you are the 'I' of yourself. Stay with it. There are no rules. And above all, *enjoy it*.

o we have to choose between finding God
and having money?

For those of you who are seekers, I have some new information. Just as you have experiments going on in your lives, so do we
on our side of the veil. And material wealth in relation to the Path
is one of them.

For centuries, seekers have asked to be excluded from material wealth because they had been taught that having wealth dis-
tracts from the goal of finding God. You have believed this long
enough. The experience that will be coming to many of you will
be one of discovering a deep desire for God can be yours *as well as*
material wealth. You will have the delightful job of learning how
well you can balance both of these. Aren't you glad? I mean this
sincerely, because your minds have programmed you against
wealth and pleasure, against things that make your eyes sparkle
and your feet dance.

It is delightful to feel all Life move through you, including
material life. Money and God will not feel separate. The challenge
will be to balance the flow. Many of you will not keep the material
gains for yourselves. There are many who, after receiving wealth
with one hand, will give it away with the other. And that is what
will be different. The new holders of wealth will be the new dis-
pensers of wealth.

Many people who now have wealth cannot give it up. For
various reasons, they need to accumulate it and keep it close. But I
ask you to consider letting go of some of your large sums of
money so there will be a vacancy for us to fill. Please understand,
the energies of the New Age are asking you to receive and to give.
It will be an exciting job some of you have waited a long time to
experience.

For a long time, seekers have gone without material things,
and in so doing, developed a poverty consciousness. Begin to turn
this kind of awareness around by stating: "I am willing to accept
and receive all the bounty this universe wants to give me, without
exception. And I will do my best to share it with consciousness

153

and responsibility." If you implant this idea deeply within your psyche, you will override those old beliefs which tell you money is evil, or you don't deserve it. Be willing to open yourself to everything this universe wants to flood into you. Be ready to receive—and then experience the joy of giving. There is nothing like it!

How do we know, out of all the suggestions about spiritual freedom given, which ones to use?

It is true that, in these past eight years, I have thrown out a lot of suggestions. The reason is very simple. Each one of you, in your own way, is absolutely unique. Through all the lives you have lived, you have accumulated knowledge and you have accumulated skills your conscious mind does not remember. My job is to remind you.

So we all throw out different ideas. And when you are paying close attention with your 'inner' being, and not listening with your 'outer' ears, you feel an upwelling when some of the ideas come your way. "I like that one. This one sounds good. Ah, yes, here is one for me." When that happens, stop looking! You have what you need. You have found your own way. Your obligation then is to apply it to your conscious life, hour after hour, day after day. What this is all about is to remind you of old and wondrous skills.

But we also want to bring you *new* and wondrous skills, because through the centuries things have changed. Your ability to pick up new information, to put your head in the stars, and keep your feet deeply planted in the earth, has grown. You have stretched. You are open in many more ways than you were, say five hundred years ago.

So there is a whole new body of information coming to you. And this is where you need to be watchful, because it can be a little tricky. Because it will be unfamiliar, usually the first response when meeting the unfamiliar is one of resistance. When you don't like what is coming at you, take it as a sign to be alert, be aware. When an edgy feeling comes instead of a sweet, smooth acceptance, oftentimes you are being hit in an area of your psyche *where you have unfinished business*!

When your whole being is engaged with 'not liking a truth,' your next statement should be, "There's something here, something real is engaging me." And then comes the difficulty of fac-

155

ing whatever it is, going through it, working with it, accepting it, and letting all the information in.

So what to do when you find yourself feeling this resistance or resentment? Sit down with yourself, open up and say, "Alright, I'm ready to listen. I'm ready." You will be amazed at the difference. Haven't you done this in your friendships? When two of you sit down and are ready to listen, all of a sudden there's no problem exchanging the information. The hard part was getting the two of you to sit down together.

But finally the magic comes. If you can just turn your perception around and be willing to sit with the uncomfortable moment, you will find everything begins to change. Something happens in the psyche when you decide to listen. It relaxes. It 'lets go.'

How do you let go? All I can say is you simply *stop* and just let go. In that moment new information flows past your barriers. And with the new information comes new wonder, new expansion, and new Life!

**I** am asking a question for a friend of mine. He has just lost his wife suddenly to cancer. He needs to know how to cope, how to get through each day, after having lost the most important person in his life.

I don't have an instant answer for your friend. One difficulty with being a human being is that, on taking physical birth, the openings to other realities close down. You find yourself crammed into a physical body looking through physical eyes and perceiving the world through the separated awarenesses of the senses. You are told from the first to the last day of your life that all you really are is a small person looking through eyes that see chaos. Most often this is how the human sees itself.

The path to freedom, peace, and harmony lies in the realization there is within this world something which tells you that you are greater than the physical body.

The difficulty for your friend is clear. He believes his wife to be only a body; himself as well. His spiritual doorways are not opened wide enough so he can see or sense she is alright. He wants to know how he can help her and what's happening on her side of the veil. These are basic questions.

The answer, my friend, is not simple. I do not know anyone who has not ached and suffered over the death of a dearly beloved one. Even the very wise and expanded pass through a time of mourning when a loved one on the physical plane leaves them. Please beg your friend to mourn boldly, and to *claim* his mourning. The least helpful thing is the stoic answer that hides feelings behind a facade and says, "I don't hurt." That kind of pain and suffering turns and goes into the body.

What I am going to say next will not please many of you. But it is my truth, and I offer it for your consideration. Hidden within the pain of the loss is the antidote to the pain! By continuing to feel the pain, it one day gives up its treasure. There *will* come a moment when your friend awakens with the *feeling* that somehow "God's in Its heaven and all is right—with me and with her." And peace then descends. Something has shifted and he will

157

feel better. The sharp pain of sorrow softens and there is more room for it to move around.

Another question that might arise in looking at the situation is this: Why, if you are masters of your own destiny, would you pick a life that has death in it? This is a very bold question. Part of the answer is it was not meant for you to run about this earth plane century after century simply enjoying the earth experience. What you have come here to understand is you are beyond *all* those small, limited parameters of being just a body. You have come to understand that you are vastly more wondrous, more powerful, alive, and compassionate than the human situation shows you to be. So death comes and it reminds you. Pain, suffering, illness, and loss all come to remind you there is some greater purpose here.

But it does not help to tell someone who is hurting that everything is happening for their own good. It is not something the heart wants to hear. The heart aches and has to be honored in its aching. And as time passes, the pain lessens and new perceptions and realizations begin to come.

So why did you program death into the earth experience? The answer is to keep reminding you this life is not the All of everything. It is only a very small part of the Whole. Compared to the capacity of the human psyche to feel and move into other states of consciousness, it is small.

The more your friend can remember death is the experience of *all* mankind, the more he will shift his focus from his personal agony and expand his awareness to a greater state of understanding. Man suffering through his own life has to know a certain amount of pain. Open the experience up to the greater understanding that this is part of mankind's *total* journey and the process becomes easier. Know the process of grieving will come to an end.

158

**W**hen the spirit leaves the body after a person dies, does it incarnate immediately? And when it does incarnate, why does it choose a particular moment?

I will ask you to share my view of life for awhile, so you can get a sense of how I see things. Then you will understand my answer. I do not believe in a linear life—like walking down a road. My observation of 'Deep Self' is that you and this moment together are a point of amazing beauty and power that is being bombarded on all sides by events, both earthly and otherworldly, past and future, and these things occur outside of what you call time-space. Together you form an incredibly deep, rich, and empowered tapestry. All parts of you are alive. A small part of you is the physical body, which you call your self. But the tapestry, my friend, is much vaster.

This small part of you is playing out a little drama in one area of this vast tapestry. Then it does what you call 'die.' Well, in truth, of course, there is no such thing. And when you ask if the spirit leaves the body, yes, in actual fact it does, because it goes back the way it came. When you were born, your 'spirit' came and locked into your body, and when you die, it unlocks and departs.

You ask if the spirit leaves immediately at death. Well, it depends. Sometimes it goes back and forth for awhile. You know how some people can't decide whether they want chocolate cake or vanilla ice cream? It's the same when they are dying. "Should I go? I don't know. Yes. No. Well, maybe." In this case, they don't decide all of a sudden. They go and they return. They do that until they feel comfortable. Then finally they decide to leave and they are gone. I am trying to make light of death because *it is fun*. You have forgotten that, but in truth you have died thousands upon thousands of times and you are still here and still willing to die again—so it can't be too bad, can it?

The decision to die is made. The body is left and the 'spirit' withdraws. The moment the 'spirit' is no longer encapsulated in a physical body, it expands. And let me assure you, this is a most wonderful feeling. It is like the 'genie in the bottle.' All of a sud-

159

den the top is off and the genie is out and fills the sky. This is what your 'spirit' feels like when you die.

Now depending on many things, eventually you begin to look around and sift through the events of your recent earth experience. And with that new view, you may realize you didn't really 'get it' that last lifetime. Because you see, what you came to the earth plane 'to get' is the knowledge you *are* Divine. You are the Godself moving through all kinds of experiences, and this *separated world is an illusion*. If you haven't 'gotten' that, you realize you cannot go past a certain level of awareness until you do! So you reach the point where you make your decision to again come into incarnation. You decide the time, the place, and the people who would be maximum, and you do it. Basically, it's as simple as that. It is simple because you are so vast and have access to the unlimited information you need to make those decisions. It is certainly a much more sophisticated and reliable process than the computers that you work with. The variables are infinite and they are all in *your* computer. You simply make the decision, based on the data you have, and you return.

I want to tell you again, not so you will run out and do it, but so you will not be so afraid. Death is a wonderful experience! Please hear this. It is much like the image of the genie getting out of the bottle. And in that expanded freedom, you are able to see many things from a vaster point of view. It's rather like the flea that walks through the rug on your living room floor. If there are eighteen colors in the rug, can you imagine what the little flea is thinking as it goes from color to color? It has no conception of what it is passing through. But then, all of a sudden, the flea takes a mighty jump. Up in the air, it looks down and says, "Look, flowers! I've got it! That's what all those colors were!" So it is with you. You jump up and out and you look down and say, "I've got it!"

Many people have recorded this experience. Carl Jung has a wonderful description in his book *Memories, Dreams, and Reflections*. When he felt himself dying, he experienced it as a movement up. It was absolutely delightful. He's sitting in a cave, just like in the movies, and there is a wonderful wise man who begins to talk

160

with him. Then, all of a sudden, whoosh! Carl Jung isn't dying anymore. He's coming back down. And lo and behold, he sees his doctor moving up while he is moving down. He returns to his body, again feeling its pain, and he is definitely angry about it. The first day he puts his feet back on the ground, his doctor dies.

You worry about death and dying, but Jung loved it. He loved the expansion, the beauty, the wonder, and the experience of it. Please, do not hasten your time of dying. But just know, for yourself and for anyone else, that in the end it is a wonderful release. And from that expanded place, you will look around and understand what you see. So do not be afraid.

have a dying patient who is a member of the church. She keeps asking, "Why is God doing this to me? Why does God hurt me?" I want to know how I can love her and help ease her before she dies.

So the question is: A patient is dying. And a very compassionate nurse wants to know how to ease such statements as, "Why is God punishing me?"

With all due respect, I am not sure there is a lot you can do for this particular person. Your speech will not change anything because her belief patterns about God are so strong. But your 'beingness' and who you are have the capacity to make changes. As you are near and touch her and help her on the physical level, you can work quietly on the inner planes, sending her the 'power of the positive.' Focus this power in whatever way comes to you, then silently transmit it. On some level she is going to grasp the change of energy.

If you go to your mind to seek answers about how to ease her, it cannot affect her. You cannot change her mind. You have already tried that. So just keep moving on the inner planes as best you can. When you think of her, put the positive in motion. What you will be doing is creating an energy field of hope, openness, and clarity, giving her the opportunity of joining with you. Whether she does or not, my friend, is her choice. Ideas won't influence her.

She has lived a lifetime with certain ingrained negative beliefs about God. And she would not consider it a service if you tried to take them away. She will not give them up, because she believes that to do so would be giving up her chance to see God. So just work silently and positively, moment by moment, and you will be doing all you can. She has a choice around receiving it, but it will overflow and there are other people who will benefit from it greatly.

What does it mean to have this illness called AIDS sweeping so terrifyingly across the world?

My dear friend, we cannot say there is only a single meaning for this particular situation. One part of the answer is to say that many people need to move into a deep understanding of *their own* sexuality—what it means to them and how they can live their lives most creatively and abundantly with this energy. So in one sense, sexuality is the issue. But not in the way the negative mind would have it.

There has to be a way for mankind, *as a whole*, to look within and ask a basic question, "How do I live my sexual life most dynamically and with the most awareness and clarity?" That the issue is sexual is obvious, and it is around AIDS it is coming into focus. It is an issue, quite frankly, that has been lying asleep for a long time. From the Victorian era, sexuality has been very regimented in this part of the world. Few people have had a chance to ask themselves what *they* think about it. They have had other people or organizations telling them what they should think.

Whenever there is a necessity to look at an area of consciousness which is buried, something like AIDS will come into creation. The physical condition known as cancer has been prevalent in recent years. Out of it has come an understanding that the medical model is not perfect, that there has to be a deep commitment on the part of each individual to decide what life is bringing to his or her body. How can you live in a way that is harmonious with your own energy field? What decisions do you need to make to keep yourself free of this condition? Until recently, the medical model was almost totally omnipotent because everyone believed in it without question. But doubt will always have to come whenever you place your power outside of yourself. *Doctors do not keep you free of cancer. You do.* On some level you all know this.

Alright then, what is the lesson about AIDS? You will find out when you begin to examine your ideas about sexuality. And beyond that, decide what it means to live your life dynamically—

becoming responsible for your choices and knowing there is always risk involved. Because sexuality falls into the physical arena, and because the end-product at this time is so horrendous, AIDS has gotten everybody's attention, just as cancer did when it first appeared.

I believe you have the capability to come up with a solution to the dilemma as far as the physical body is concerned. So instead of moving into fear, *watch* what is happening. People who move into fear *move into exclusion*. Many difficult things are surfacing because of Aids, and you are going to have to start addressing the issues beyond the sexual realm. For example: the fear of children in the schools catching AIDS from a schoolmate. Is it realistic? Is it not? There are many judgments around the segment of the population manifesting this illness. Where do you stand with *your* judgments? Many such things are being brought into question. Please do not be simplistic and say, "AIDS means so and so for this planet." The question is: What does it mean for you? Ask yourself what deep fears it brings up in your psyche. Take the responsibility of asking yourself, "What do I feel? What do I intend to do in my life around this question?"

There has always been some major movement in the world that takes away life. Cancer is terrible, but the understanding of it is now different because clarification is beginning to unfold. New, dynamic choices are being made around this disease. I am not saying it is wonderful cancer is here. I am simply observing there are *victorious ways to deal with all the difficulties* that come onto your planet. And I feel you must take the responsibility for discovering what perceptions and fears the issue of AIDS brings up for you so you can be victorious. Start dealing with them on your own. If you want to help the whole situation, you can help best by understanding what it all means to you.

There is another part of the question to bring forward here, and it is this. Why are so many alive, vital people suddenly dying? I realize, from your perception, death can be a very negative issue. But I would like to remind you of something you already know. Death can be a moment of absolute heroic wonder, beauty, and clarity *when experienced from an empowered position.*

164

Tasteless as it is, war is one opportunity to experience death from an empowered position. There is no overt war going on now for your country. Please understand, *as a positive statement*, there have to be ways for young people to die. There has to be a victorious way for young people to leave the earth plane. Outside of suicide and war, what is left are accidents and illnesses, which have always been here and always will be, in one form or another.

Death remains an opportunity. I understand the agony and I know how it feels, but an entity chooses to die when it realizes the maximum moment for death is *appropriate*. There is a time when all things move into equilibrium and death is best. The momentum is maximum for doing what needs to be done. The mental, the physical, and the emotional are in a state of readiness and the necessity is there. And the willing choice is made on a deep level.

Someone walks down the street and a brick drops on his head. You wonder if it is a caprice. But no, there is an inner knowing of the appropriateness of that action. For those left behind, it looks dismal or difficult. Nevertheless, people choose what is available out of the repertoire of choices. I don't mean to be simplistic, but there are only a certain number of choices. When the whole entity says it's time to go, it looks around and picks a way. When it is not necessary to stay, staying is inappropriate. Painful, but correct.

Never say someone dies to help someone else. That is not the truth. A consciousness dies because it is time. You will know this directly when you start to die. You will say, "I am not dying so only that person can benefit. I am dying because I need to, because there are certain things in my mechanism that say it is time. The off-ramp is present and I am going."

You look around and make your choice—lightning or something equally as dramatic. You take what's there, what is available, *what will teach you*. And you pick from the choices of mankind. A lot of people who are dying of AIDS are dying victoriously, with a tremendous amount of power. There *will be a solution*, a cure, at which time the intensity of this opportunity will no longer be available.

165

So if you look at it from the positive side, you will see that people need to have creative choices on how to leave this planet. It is empowering to say, "I've got five months to live—and I am going to live like a warrior. I am going to get my life in order. I am going to be powerfully alive to the end." That is a dynamic and aware way to die. When the cure comes, people will get well and other opportunities will have to present themselves. Right now it is a victorious choice for many people.

In another interview, Bartholomew gave us the following view of the AIDS situation: It is fashionable today to say that AIDS is God's punishment against those practicing male homosexuality. I would present another point of view for your consideration: Is it not possible the message to the western world at large is to examine their judgments against a minority, and to ask if it might be this very *judgment* that has put the minority in a weakened state and thereby susceptible to dis-ease? Since it is a *sexual judgment*, would it not be in the sexual arena that such dis-ease would manifest? Is it possible this need not have happened if compassion and understanding had been present rather than isolation and condemnation? If you wish to participate in finding a 'cure' for a situation whose roots involve all of mankind, consider working deeply on removing those pieces of judgment on this issue that reside in *your* mind. Such is the nature of true service to mankind.

I feel that I have accepted the responsibility for my own choices around disease and death. But what about animals? How can I reconcile the diseases they get? Do they have their own choices of disease or do they pick them up from their owners?

This question was asked by a veterinarian. —Ed.

You have a sense of your own free will. You choose to be born in a large city rather than a rural area. Now give that same power to the animal kingdom. There is a definite difference between the animal consciousness which chooses to be born and live in the wild, and one which chooses to be domesticated and live with human consciousness.

One of the things the animal kingdom is trying to do through living with you is to expand their capacity to 'feel.' Just as is all of Creation, they are trying to become Vaster. Not bigger animals, but Vaster. They want to move into different kinds of experiences. And one of the experiences they wish to feel is that of empathy, or sympathetic understanding between the animals and the humans they choose to live with. That 'empathetic' experience of the domesticated animal is not the same as the experience of the one in the wild, who has different decisions to make.

When you have an animal living with you, you really have no idea of what you are getting from them. As you 'train' them, you are also being trained. Animals are constantly training humans. It isn't as though the human consciousness is going one way and the animal consciousness another. They learn each from the other, and sometimes the animal is the more willing student.

As a byproduct of this experiment in empathy, animals know they can begin to resonate to some of the beliefs their human companions have and, in the body, this means they are subject to diseases of the human psyche they would not get in the wild. It is also through their empathy with humans that they *consciously* make, at times, the decision to absorb some of the human illnesses into their bodies. An animal's body deals differently with disease and pain than does the human. In their natural acceptance of these

167

difficulties, they suffer less than their human counterparts.

So please remember, *animals make choices of conscious expansion*. And part of that experience is being with the human kingdom. They love it. Just realize it is a beautiful trade-off for them, and they do not begrudge the price. They would not have selected it otherwise.

So participate with them. Enjoy each other. Acknowledge the animal kingdom is getting what it came to get. And if they receive something that isn't quite as exciting as they would like, they understand. They have an *intuitive* knowingness the experience with you is appropriate and they join with it joyfully. So honor their choice and do the best you can from your side. Animals forms are making wonderful, expansive changes. They are master teachers in the natural world. And I thank you for this question on their behalf.

hy are children born handicapped? And should we try to heal them?

As part of experiencing you are all One, that all of life is One, there is a necessity for you to grapple with certain major 'givens' the human condition has to offer. One of these is being born handicapped or becoming handicapped during your lifetime. Where I disagree with most of you is when you make this a negative condition by assuming a handicapped child or person has done something wrong in the past that it must now atone for.

It is my perception that, most of the time, the ones who come in with a handicap come with the courage and determination to bring into that situation as much love, light, power and beauty as they can. They shine as victorious examples, when they are successful. And the one thing they do not need is your pity. How dare they be given pity when they come as the warriors to show, in the midst of incredible limitations, that they can give to the world the very qualities the Christos embodied. What I think they deserve is applause.

Should you try to heal them? Absolutely. Some of you say a certain affliction has come to someone because of their karma, so there is no need for them to do anything about it. Yet, if such a one is in your life, wherein lies *your* karma? No one just drops into your life without reason. There is always a place where they fit. So when a handicapped child is present, the question is presented, "What does this have to do with me?" And most of the time it has to do with your ability to take care of that being with humor, acceptance, compassion, and determination. Acceptance when it's inconvenient, and humor in the face of frustration, simply allowing the wonderful feeling of rapport to continue to move between you, keeping alive all their beauty and wonder. Please understand, there is much more going on than is apparent to you. If you can remember you are more than just your body, you will remember *they* are too! Keep the vastness of your essence moving between the two of you.

169

No physical affliction bothers anyone as much as does the feeling of being different, separate and somehow outside of life. That is the greatest pain. Your job my friends, is to remove the feeling of separation by blending your awareness with theirs. Bring them into you; don't push them away by being embarrassed to look at them. Look in their faces, into their eyes, and right into their Being. *And let them see you.* Those are the moments to give of yourself totally. So they in return will know you recognize there is only 'One,' and that they are carrying their part of the whole while you are carrying yours.

This is a subject that I have received many inquiries about. It is also a subject that is going to be difficult for a lot of you. The moment I mention it, a great many of you will rush to one position and a great many will rush to the opposite position. There will be very few left in the middle. But I ask you to suspend your judgments and see what you can learn. The question is: Is the drug Ecstasy usable for spiritual development and for harmonizing relationships?

I am not your keeper, I am your brother. Since the question was raised, I will simply tell you what I perceive to be the reality about this kind of experience and then suggest you make your choices out of that. *I am not going to take a stand.* I am simply going to present, for your awareness, what happens in and around the physical body after a drug has been ingested.

The first and most obvious point is the observation that your bodies are not all the same. Therefore, whether something like this drug Ecstasy is usable to you or not depends on *your* understanding of *your own* physical body. The other very obvious thing to point out is that drugs change the physical body. One thing helpful with the passage of this drug through the system is water. It helps prevent having the drug trapped in the body where it can cause difficulties.

Those of you who feel very opposed to these substances, please entertain the possibility that somewhere in your past incarnative patterns you may have misused them. When someone who is very adamantly against a drug is presented with that substance, their whole internal system shuts down. If this is your experience, stand on what you feel is appropriate *for you* and do not talk yourself or let anyone else talk you into using it. Your response is your own and to go against it could present you with great physical difficulties. At the same time, please give *freedom of choice to others*, because some of you will, in turn, have the immediate desire to try the substance.

My understanding is that Ecstasy is brand new, and has

helped create the category of 'designer drug.' What a wonderful phrase! It is 'designed' for a new and specific purpose and therefore not relevant to the past. Ever since you first woke up on the earth plane and felt stuck here, you have been looking for ways to escape the limitations of being in a body without dying. Some of you fell into lifetimes of taking the 'easy' way out. Ways such as tobacco, alcohol, sex, and drugs gave you a quick way to slip past the limited body, so these methods became familiar.

Let us look at what happens during a drug experience. When you ingest anything into your system, you open up areas that have long been closed, many through fear. It does not make much sense for you to ingest a drug that increases your fear, when fear is already your problem. And some of these drugs are absolutely fear-producing. It is their job to blast open as many centers as possible, and to present the hidden material in one overwhelming experience. It is not surprising that a manifestation of this is what you call a 'negative trip.'

Some drugs have as their job the soft and gentle opening of a specific center. This particular drug, Ecstasy, happens to be one of these. Now, does that mean it is totally harmless? My friends, *nothing* is totally harmless. Do I recommend it? I neither recommend it nor condemn it. I ask you to understand that drugs blast open a part of your energy field which you could open on your own if you had the determination to do so. The difficulty with drugs, my friends, is they make you lazy. It is easy to swallow them and have an uplifting experience, but basically they make you lazy.

In the old times, a part of the initiation ritual was the ingestion of certain *natural* substances. The 'shaman' used these substances to help the 'initiate' understand different levels of consciousness. But we are talking about a controlled environment, where the person administering the substance, or the sacrament, knew exactly what would happen. They could follow the journey of the initiate and therefore rescue them if necessary. Are there a lot of shamans around today? No, there are not. So you have to act as your own and surround yourself with an environment you can trust.

172

When the drug hits your system, it opens things up and gives you a momentary glimpse of a different 'reality.' At this point things become difficult. Your mind tells you the drug has given you an experience that cannot be repeated without the drug. This is not true! Because any opening you have, in what you call an altered state, is also available to you in the natural state. Please understand, those experiences do not occur only when you ingest something outside of your system. When you have ignited that opening and seen what is there, it is up to you to find out if the state you have experienced is real by activating it on your own. This is why, in times past, most people were not allowed to take the sacraments. *They were not willing to do the work of bringing that state of awareness into their lives day after day.*

Those of you who use these substances like the altered state, but often don't wish to go through the discipline necessary to truly bring it into your life. The only prayer to ask while *on the drug* is to be shown how to have the experience at other times. Allow that open state to be the teacher. Find the path that does not depend on the drug, and then go on with your life. When you are given information, you are responsible for acting as though you had it! The drug experience is confusing because most of you do not accept that responsibility.

So do exactly what you want. You will anyway. But be alive and conscious of what you are looking for. If you choose to use this drug, be aware it is your intention that is important. What your intention is will tell you exactly where you are going to end up. Those of you who use it to stimulate the 'lower' centers will end up with a 'lower' experience. No matter what you do my friends, as in everything, *your intention is all.*

Even if you are one of those who uses this drug Ecstasy to harmonize your relationships, my statement is still the same. Find out what the pattern is that allows you to have harmony in your relationships, then start doing it without the drug. *Do not get dependent on something outside yourself to give you the experiences you are looking for.* Be alive and aware of what you are doing.

I repeat, anything you can do with this drug you can do without it. No one gets to leave this planet until they learn it is possible to get 'high' on Life itself, with the sheer joy of living, a moment to moment delight. When you know that, it means you have opened up all the parts of your Being and allowed the Divine to move through you so clearly you just feel the delight. Filled with the Light. In the end, living, moving, and having your Being right here, in its own natural state, is very addictive. I suggest you get addicted to *Life*! It is one thing you can't get rid of.

n relationship, is one person's purpose more important than another's?

A person's purpose in life is not a happy relationship. The purpose is to become whole within yourself, to know you are capable of amazing things, and to know you have the courage and ability to go out and do them. But none of this will happen until you believe, deeply inside yourself, *you are worth it.*

Every one of you is different. Your lives are different, your feelings are different, your vibrations, your thoughts, your desires, your needs, your understandings, the way you view the world— they're all different. So when you talk about coming together on the path, the inference is you must both fit perfectly or it won't work. But my friends, since that is not true, you are either going to be alone a long time or very unhappy until you release that concept.

What is relationship about? It is about two people with different frequencies who have enough similarities to be drawn together. And if you are drawn together in a very strong and impacted way, you experience what you call 'falling in love.' *Falling* in love sounds very dangerous to me.

But it is true, when you are attracted to someone, a lot of your energy fields have points of contact. So you feel secure or excited, interested, delighted, or any of the other emotions you experience upon falling in love. These factors bring you together. But then comes what I would call the deeper reason for your being together. And now I am not just talking about love affairs. The same thing happens with friends and others you care about. You meet them—explosion! And as the relationship deepens, you begin to run into what I call the 'other strands' of your energy fields that need to be worked on.

Please hear this. Whenever you run up against feelings of jealousy, possessiveness, envy, anger, whatever it might be, *your* system should sound the alarm. Be aware you are now in the presence of one of *your* unfinished areas. Do not say, "Look at what

175

they are doing. I would be so happy if *they* would stop. It's *their* problem, so why don't *they* change!"

With a little humor, you can begin to face in yourself all the areas that need to be smoothed out. Smoothing out in relationships can be done simply. First step: Claim 100% responsibility. If you feel jealous, it is not because something *out there* made you jealous. It may be that something *has* happened out there, but the fact is something *in you* has responded. At the very moment when you are filled and absorbed with the feeling of jealousy comes the point of choice. Find out what any feeling is saying about *you*.

Jealousy indicates someone has something you want and don't have. The answer is to *get it for yourself*—not to demand the other person give it to you. And I am not speaking about material objects here. I am talking about your internal issues of peace, happiness, and safety.

There are many different parts to the psyche that need to be seen and dealt with. When you take the projections of those parts off the person in front of you and bring them back inside yourself, you will find *you can get what you want*. It's something inside *yourself* you want so badly. A simple way to become whole is to continually ask yourself, "What can I do, right now, for myself, that will make a difference?" So we end where we began. Nothing will change until you begin to believe that you are worth more than you are now getting. Your purpose in life is to become whole. If the other person in your life really loves you, they will want for you those things you deeply want for yourself and you will want the same for them. Then your purpose in life will be mutual; no hierarchies, just good company on the journey Home.

ow does one deal with the feelings that arise when one feels betrayed by someone they trusted for many years?

The first thing to do is acknowledge your anger, your rage, and your pain. You allow yourself the full range of good feelings, but when what you call the 'negative ones' surface, out comes resistance. Through past conditioning, feelings of anger, hostility, or betrayal have been judged unacceptable. But, my friend, you must make the honest admission you are feeling what you are feeling. Stay within the confines of your own psyche, acknowledge the feelings, and get them moving.

Then, as you allow these strong feelings their full expression, say to yourself, "In the midst of this anger, I love myself. In the midst of this pain, *I* love myself right now." You have felt the betrayal, but also a sense of yourself as not being big enough to fly above it. There is a part of you that judges your responses as negative and therefore wrong. In those moments of judgment, *you do not love yourself.*

But I ask you to understand you are human. You are in a physical body and have an emotional body. And the job of the emotional body is to feel emotions. Acknowledging your emotions does not mean you have to act out of them. In allowing yourself to feel your emotions, you will begin to feel vaster. You will start feeling more acceptable to yourself, more whole, and eventually you will come into balance with your feelings around the event.

Q: Should I approach this person who has betrayed me? I would like to vent my feelings and let this person know them.

My friend, *you* have to decide. But look carefully at your motive before you ever go to anyone with this kind of thing in mind. Ask yourself if you want to let them have it because you are hurt *or* do you really want to clear up the situation, *or* is it a little bit of both? Your decision will come from this process. But whatever you do, *be responsible* for your actions. Please realize, whatever you set in motion *you'll have to live with*. If you find your motive to be vengeful, please stop and think about it again. Because that's

177

how karma gets started or is perpetuated. You get hurt, you hurt them, they hurt you back, and so it goes endlessly. It's got to stop somewhere. So think about it. You can 'vent' your feelings toward the person *in absentia*—meaning that he or she doesn't have to be sitting in your living room. You *can* get your deepest feelings out without having the physical person there to receive them.

It's part of the human condition to feel emotional pain. Someone recently asked me, "How can humans ever really love other humans when they are so accustomed to being betrayed?" The only answer I have is that the love you are talking about comes and goes, so it will continue to be painful until you begin bringing in the Love of the Divine. Until you get *impersonal* love moving in your life, you will keep on being hurt. That's just the way of it.

Please realize what the human condition is all about, and try not to look to the small kind of a love affair to give you the feeling you are really looking for. The human love affair is a mirror of the feeling of Divine Love. And the Love of the Divine is not limited to one other person. The question it all comes down to is—how can you find and live Divine Love? That is truly the only question.

Would you address the issue of fear? In relationships of any kind, whether personal or business, I find there is love and compassion, but occasionally an insidious distrust comes up that spoils it.

Good question, thank you. Simply stated again, the question is: No matter what you do, no matter how loving you want to be, there are times when you fall into fear. Falling into fear, you then behave in a way that increases your fear, because you begin to do all the paranoid things that make other people act fearfully as well. This then increases your belief in fear, so it goes around and around. Now, how do you stop it?

There is only one way I have ever seen to truly stop a process and it begins with paying close attention to it, and really *feeling* it in your body. You know, my friends, when you have a physical ailment, you go to a lot of trouble to get well. The first thing you do is put yourself to bed. You announce to the world you have to take care of yourself, and you begin to build your health back again. If you would take the same care and interest when you have a 'fear ailment,' you would begin to understand where it came from and what it wants from you. Then you can let it go. Fear is an energy that can be your teacher—if you have the willingness to face it.

Fear is power. It is an energy that is easily felt. It is a part of the life-cycle. When fear is with you, you can train yourself to say, "My friend, you are here! I remember you well. You have come to tell me some part of me needs looking at, needs explaining. I am going to sit with you, my friend fear, until you disclose your secret to me."

If you will address fear as something real and helpful, rather than frustrating and terrifying, you will have finished with a great deal of the problem. Please understand, energy *will* talk to you. It will talk plainly to you through dreams, images, symbols; through visions, ideas, and promptings. It will talk to you in a way you can understand.

I would like to present one way to increase your familiarity

179

with this energy. Have a dialogue with it. Sit and ask the following questions: What color is it? What shape? Where in the body does it dwell? What makes it larger? Smaller? What started it? *Who* comes to mind as you work with this fear? *What* events bubble up? What do you feel like doing? And finally, what will it take to calm this energy down? Ask it—what do you need to become calm and relaxed?

So, when you are in fear remember, *anything* that comes to you is your friend, whether it's nightmare or terror. If you can see it as energy approaching in order to solve a basic dilemma, you will be able to appreciate it and let the fear approach with love and caring. And something very strange happens. You begin to *want* to experience fear. And when you want to experience it, you know the game is almost over, because you are now ready to finish the unfinished process within you. When that moment comes, things are really under way!

**W**hat is the highest octave and purpose of sex? If everything is to be used to 'journey Home,' how can we use the sexual act to help?

To understand what I am about to say, please keep in mind that you are all energy in motion. You constantly vibrate who you are to the world around you and people are constantly picking up the essence of who you are. You don't fool anybody and they don't fool you. If you choose to be fooled, it is because there is another kind of game you want to be playing, so you choose to play it and keep yourself hidden. No person who is having a love affair outside their main relationship ever fools the other person, because their energy field is constantly giving off that message.

The sexual act itself changes your energy field. It blends and merges on a very deep level with the energy of your partner. So, the first and last question you should ask yourself before entering into the sexual act is, "Do I want to have as part of my life, my experience, my feeling tone, the essence of this person?" If the answer is yes, then I suggest you enjoy it. If the answer is not yes, then I ask you to reconsider.

I am speaking very seriously and very directly. In the sexual blending, you take into yourself more of each other's essence than in any other way on the human plane. This is why it is so attractive. Sexuality is not attractive only because it is pleasurable. It is attractive because, for a few moments in time-space, you know you can blend with another human being. You are added unto, you are filled. You become vaster. You are not alone. Blending takes place when two people care about one another. And sexual energy does not always come from the sexual act.

There are great sciences devoted to using sexuality to reach realization. One is called Tantric Yoga. Those of you who are interested, by all means use it. Just remember, in the coming together, you are sharing someone else's power, someone else's wonder. When two or more are gathered together, magic happens, whether it be sexuality, praying, walking, or dying. Everything can become greater.

181

As with any magic, you have to choose whether or not to perform it. Sexuality is a very empowering device, properly used—which means with awareness, and I am not talking about skill, I am talking about awareness. It can be used to the betterment of both consciousnesses. As you enter into the act, please ask that it be used to empower you both in the deepest way possible. This increases the *awareness* of this empowering action. Then you blend *with your own Being* as well as with the essence and wonder of another. By making aware choices, sexuality can be the path that takes you Home.

What has happened to the peace, joy, and love between the people of the world?

When energy increases, whether it is a boost in vibration or in response to a call for help, it does not increase only the positive aspects of the planetary system. If this were so, things would be a lot easier. But when energy enters and is present, it activates all things in equal measure. Just as the sun shines everywhere, energy penetrates everything. So whatever seems to be in the shadows will increase and whatever seems to be in the light will also increase.

My friends, there is not much to do when you observe the dark shadow side increasing. Merely activate, with increasing power, your own light side, day after day. You cannot stop the increase of polarities. They increase together, but that is not a dismaying statement. It is a statement of freedom, because eventually you will understand, the more you are committed to increasing the power within yourself, the more you will know that no matter how difficult things appear, everything is going in the right direction.

It is true there are many people on the earth plane who could be considered 'young souls.' So be it. Let them do what young souls do. In the doing, they will learn. It is certainly not your job to criticize them. It is simply your job to do your utmost to understand and accept yourself, as your own soul moves through different layers of understanding. In that expansion, you will come to do what is needful for your awareness and let others do what they need to. And please refrain from that strange judgmental statement that says, "Be different than you are." You did not all come at the same time. You will not all leave at the same time. So, be conscious of the soul's unfoldment. Give compassion to your younger brothers and sisters who are doing the best they can to learn what they need to learn.

Q: How can I empower my life? I don't like feeling weak and helpless.

If you decide to live your life as a warrior, which is necessary when you wish to empower yourself, it means you must find ways to expand your own awareness, your own light, power, and wonder, to such an extent that events which used to make you feel helpless no longer touch you. Even, for example, when the body is filled with pain, the answer is the same. Expand your consciousness past the boundaries that you are used to, and what happens as a byproduct is your physical vehicle also begins to go through changes. You cannot change the energy within yourself without changing the cellular structure that inhabits the body form. And when you begin to transmute energy, your entire environment starts to change.

Please realize, as your life begins to change and you expand your own consciousness, you will start feeling 'up' instead of 'down,' so be ready, because there are people who are just not willing to go 'up' with you. They are going to get uncomfortable. And in their discomfort, they may decide you are too uncomfortable for them and they need something else. It's at this point you have to trust that what you are doing is maximum. And it will be hard. I say this because I honestly feel those of you who choose the Light are going to have to give up what might seem important to you at the time. In increasing the light within, be aware that *whatever you move away from cannot decrease it.* The next step is always more light-filled, but there is a time of transition to pass through which is difficult.

There are various ways to increase your power. The oldest one, which many dislike, is meditation. Because meditation, you see, means you have to sit down and shut up. There is no one to play with and no one to talk to. And there certainly is no one to report to. You just sit there and hang around and wait for God to start talking to you. This can be very boring. But it is true, if you are willing to sit through those excruciating first months, there does come a settling down. There does come a moment when your inner being is so quiet and still that another state of awareness presents itself and begins to talk to you in a direct, intimate, and ongoing way.

Another method to increase your power, which is very delightful, is through dreams. The Divine has always talked to

184

man through the dream state. If you are confused and your life seems to be dark, my suggestion is that you begin to record your dreams. Since ancient times, man has received two similar types of communication from God: visions and dreams. Through them, you can get the messages you need. You do have the wisdom, and dwelling on the meaning of dreams can bring you to amazing clarity.

Do not ignore those dreams you think of as negative. Every time you have a dream of intense negativity, instead of running away from it, I ask you to sit with it. Consider the dream as a friend and be willing to enter into the energy of it so it can teach you. Dreams are energy impinging on you when you are in a state of sleep, when your defenses are down, when your ego is not at its fullest power, when there is a chance to slide through the veil and come up on the other side and talk.

The more fearful the dream, the more pleased you should be. Fearful dreams come to you when you have enough power to deal with the issue involved, and not before. In going back to the dream in your conscious state, you have the ability to join again with the energy that is trying to teach you. You have the ability to go back through the doorway in the waking state and ask the different parts of your dream, "What were you trying to tell me? Who are you? What are you doing in there? Why did you come? What is it all about? Please teach me."

Be in control of your journey. Anyone who knows they are in control is able to move with greater ease, no matter how difficult the road. When you think you do not have control, you get very nervous. And most people on this planet today are very nervous. You do not need to be. If you do not know what to do, there are dream states, there are meditation states, and another state which is perhaps the hardest of all to acknowledge—the realization that you create your own reality. You create your reality through the belief systems and thoughts you send out. *What you think today, you live tomorrow*. If you want to know why your life is as it is, I suggest you try the writing exercise. Spend six hours, without stopping, writing every thought that comes into your mind. And you will see yourself endlessly and repeatedly go

185

through the same mentalizations over and over again in those six hours.

Two things will happen as a result of this exercise. One is a decision to end the trivia, the weighing and measuring, and judgment that runs your life. The second thing you will glimpse is the realization you have created your experiences by the *thoughts* you have held in your mind. You have drawn to you the kinds of people you think you deserve and the life experiences you think you ought to have. Endlessly in those six hours you will have revelatory experiences.

As you begin to understand the incredible power you have in creating your own reality, you can change your opinion of how you want to live. You can stop allowing the drifts of consciousness which bring up the greatest difficulties. *The hardest thing to do is to stay in the moment*! Stay perfectly conscious of everything that is happening to you, inside and out, in this moment. Pay attention to what is going on, now! When you do, you will live tomorrow what you are drifting through today.

It is in the moment you become Master of your life. Until then, the mind takes you wherever *it* wants to go. When you *know* you stand at a point of choice, you can consciously make your decisions. If you do not take control of your awareness, your unconscious mind will. And do you really want to live your life with the choices your unconscious makes? I don't think so. When you take responsibility for what is happening, there comes a moment when you know *you* have created it and you decide to create it in a way you can delight in. Your absolute birthright IS to create a life that makes you happy. God wants happiness—pure, exuberant, endless, empowered, dynamic, creative happiness, for all!

186

B A R T H O L O M E W ' S
V O C A B U L A R Y

Bartholomew sometimes uses words in a context that changes their meanings. 'He' also has a tendency to make up new words in an attempt to convey new ideas and concepts. The following vocabulary is our attempt to clarify these new words and phrases.

luck; joy

BARTHOLOMEW'S VOCABULARY

asleep - not paying attention; distracted by the outer world; not awakening to the Within

astral - the plane of existence just above the earth plane experienced frequently in dreams, nightmares, etc.

Avatar - an Enlightened One who embodies the Truth and the Light without distortion (Christ, Buddha, etc.)

Being - the essence of who you are; God, Love, the Source of all

cosmological razzle-dazzle - talking about cosmological things that rarely have anything to do with changing the quality of our life; philosophizing about reality rather than experiencing it

cosmology - the attempt to express philosophically the nature of reality; the discussion of cosmic and vast issues rather than personal, experiential ones

Deep Self - the Being of us, the One, the Source

Deva - the East Indian word for an Angelic Being

discouragement committee - frightened egos who would take away your courage to try something new

ego - the small self which views itself as separate from others

elemental kingdom - energies on a different path of evolution, the 'little people'

energy field - a power that is around and through physical forms

Enlightenment - the state of consciousness when we know what Reality is, Who we really are; God-Realization, Impersonal Love, and true Wisdom

feeling tone - the way we perceive energy inside of our bodies

finned creatures - our brothers who live in the sea

Freedom - that state of expanded consciousness characterized by a feeling of breaking loose from the chains of illusion into the Vastness; from limitations to no limitations

189

Gods - vast vortexes of energy dedicated to helping mankind

Godself - the One Universal Being from which all manifest creation comes and eventually returns

go within - take our consciousness off the outer world and become still and aware of what is going on inside us

gridwork - the network of our perceptions and misconceptions, ideas, beliefs, and fears; concretized ideas about the way our world is

grounded - realistic feelings about the earth plane and its duality by knowing how to move through it, feeling energy coming in and going through; a state of being centered within one's being

humbug - projections and judgments we place on others

implosion - an emotional or mental explosion inward, into the body

inroads - new pathways, usually in the body, to receive energy of a higher vibration

interface - the connection between two seemingly separate things or realities, the place where these two touch

journey Home - the journey to Enlightenment, to God-Knowledge, to true Reality

mandala - a usually circular piece of art or a drawing representing symbols of a higher level of reality

outrider - a person in a group that moves out from it to explore new territory in the form of new experiences, and brings it back to the group; a part of you that moves out to explore new experiences and brings it back to the rest of your psyche

(the) Path - whatever you are doing in hopes of finding God, the Self, or the One

permeable - capable of being penetrated; referring to the state of receptivity or porousness of an individual's energy field

physical vehicle - the body

process - "you can trust the process" means the path you are following consciously or unconsciously toward the goal; also, the Divine unfoldment through you

190

projection - mistaking your view of things or people for reality; putting all of those things about yourself that you don't like outside of yourself and making them attributes of other people

psyche - a Greek word meaning that part of the individual consciousness which survives death, including the many levels of our awareness that we may not be conscious of

receptor - that which receives something, usually, in this text, meaning a physical body

self - that part of us that says, "I am separate from others"

Self - see Deep Self, Godself; it is the One out of which all arises and into which all falls back into

(the) Source - that which is beyond the illusion of separation; God; The Divine; The Original One

sweat lodge - the North American Indian process whereby a group of people sit in an enclosed space in the center of which there are hot rocks and, through the aid of each other, the steam and the rocks, attempt to release their perceptions of their limitations and come to a deep understanding of Who they really are

Universal Law - Divine Truth that is as it is perceived through pattern and regularity

universal mandala - the television

Vastness - reality beyond the limits of our perception; the unfiltered state of consciousness where we know we are "All"

wake up - to realize Who you are; to awaken to the God within; to become conscious of all that is going on within your awareness

warrior - someone who has chosen to turn away from the rules of others and look for the rules only within himself/herself; one who is willing to risk being 'different' in order to be himself/herself; one who is willing to risk all in order to know God

windy spook - Bartholomew as he refers to himself in jest

winged ones - the birds

You have not undertaken the attempt to break through the illusory state into a higher understanding of consciousness for yourself alone. You do it for the millions of people who would never dream of attempting such a feat because it is not yet their time. So those of you who are the 'outriders,' be aware you come for them as well as for yourselves. And we are very grateful you do. It is only through the physical form, yourselves, that we can place any of *our* understanding into the world. Unless you are willing to be the vessels that receive such understanding, it cannot make any impact. So when you break through to any kind of deeper understanding, whether or not you ever repeat a word of what you learned, experienced, or enjoyed, doesn't matter. The experience is a part of you and you can never be separated from it. Every thing you do, every act you perform, every idea you formulate, makes a difference.

So, from my side—whatever that means, to your side—whatever that means, my endless gratitude. But most of all, something I hope you feel and do believe, my endless love. I say again, it is my great pleasure to serve you. It is also my great delight when you serve me. After all, that's what it is about, giving with one hand and receiving with the other.

Some of you I will never 'see' again, but that does not mean our love will not be joined. And to those of you that I will, until next we meet, remember please Who You Are! Never forget *Who You Are*. You are it All. You are not limitation. You are not a confused mistake. You are a vast, brilliant, extending, creative energy field that exploded out of the Heart of the One and is delighting in its journey Home. And it is my great joy to journey with you.

ॐ **Bartholomew**

Since there is
no hierarchy of Life,
this book is dedicated
with Love, to
O S O
the mesa dog.

NOTES